# NO-SEW DECORATING

# NO-SEW DECORATING

## Janet Roda

A DELTA BOOK

A DELTA BOOK

Published by
Dell Publishing Co., Inc.
1 Dag Hammarskjold Plaza
New York, New York 10017

*The photographs on the following pages
are courtesy of WestPoint Pepperell:*
1, 6, 13, 20, 24, 35, 42, 51, 59

Delta ® TM 755118,
Dell Publishing Co., Inc.

Printed in the United States of America

First printing—April 1981

**Library of Congress Cataloging in Publication Data**

Roda, Janet E.
No-sew decorating.

(A Delta book)
1. House furnishings.   2. Interior decorating—
Amateurs' manuals. I. Title.
TT387.R62      747'.9      80-26684

ISBN 0-440-56207-4

# Acknowledgments

My sincere thanks to my family and close friends for their continuous support and patience. And my special thanks to the following manufacturers for their generous contributions of supplies for the model projects:

**Stacy Fabrics**
**West Point Pepperell**
**William E. Wright Co.**

*Photographer:* **Ralph Bogertman**
*Illustrator:* **Miriam Mermelstein**
*Project Testing:* **Christine Bottomley**
*Set Design/Fabrications:* **Michael Jean Spaeth**
**William Walter**
*Book Design:* **Giorgetta Bell McRee**

# Contents

# Introduction

"No-sew decorating" is just what the title implies, the fine and fun art of using fabrics to decorate your home with the help of staples, glue, fusible bonding web, pushpins, T-pins, nails—but no sewing.

As you discover how easy it is to create and decorate entire room situations, I hope that the ideas you learn from the pages in this book will lead you on to other ideas—all your own. You bought this book because you have imagination, and I want to "trigger" that imagination to lead you into a world filled with beautiful fabrics translated into designs for living.

Decorating is not hard. It's just that some people have more of a talent for it than others—like cooking. There are good cooks and there are bad cooks, but *anyone* can cook. The same principle applies to decorating. With no-sew decorating, however, you are practically guaranteed to come out a winner. In decorating it's the effect that counts, and throughout the following pages you'll see exactly how to achieve the "effect" all by yourself—quickly and easily.

Look at a room, see what's in it—really see what is in it and you'll realize that a lot of what you are "seeing" made of fabric can be done with no sewing. As a matter of fact, every room in your home probably contains items that can easily be transformed into no-sew decorating projects. With that thought in mind I have taken a typical house, wandered through its rooms, selected those of major importance, and have created room situations filled with no-sew projects you can use in them. There are also a number of individual no-sew projects that can be used as accents in your completed rooms or created as fast, easy-to-make presents for someone special or for anyone just starting out and living on their own.

All of the projects in this book are relatively simple to do. Just take your time and think out each carefully. The wonderful thing is that if you do make a mistake (and who doesn't now and then!), there are never any sewn stitches to laboriously rip out. Simply pull out a few staples, unglue, or unfuse, all with a mere flick of your wrist.

After you try a project and see how fast and easy no-sew decorating can be, you'll want to try another and another and another. Be careful though. Decorating your home the no-sew way can become a disease—the more you do, the more you'll want to do and the more often you'll want to do it!

And finally, a word about sheets. Decorating with sheets is a very popular method of updating a room. As a matter of fact, it's so popular that I wanted to show you how beautiful and easy it is to work with them. Therefore, a majority of room situations in this book are totally done with sheets. Going through the photographs you can see how truly versatile they are. Because they can fit into any decorating situation you may have, sheets offer tremendous design variation and durability. They are particularly ideal for projects requiring wide width, such as covering walls and making draperies or curtains. Below is a yardage equivalency chart for your convenience.

# FINISHED SHEET SIZES

Twin Flat Sheet—66 × 96 = approximately 4½ yards of 36″ wide fabric

Double Flat Sheet—81 × 96 = approximately 5½ yards of 36″ wide fabric

Queen Flat Sheet—90 × 102 = approximately 6½ yards of 36″ wide fabric

King Flat Sheet—108 × 102 = approximately 8 yards of 36″ wide fabric

Regular Pillowcase—20 × 30 = approximately ¾ yards of 36″ wide fabric

King-Size Pillowcase—20 × 40 = approximately 1 yard of 36″ wide fabric

Bath Towel—27 × 50 = approximately 1 yard of 36″ wide fabric

## THOUGHTS TO KEEP IN MIND

This is not a building book, but one of decorating with fabric. Therefore, if necessary, consult your local lumberyard whenever plywood and pine are mentioned for a project.

When nailing a wood project to the ceiling or to the wall, be absolutely sure of what you are doing, especially with ceilings. Always secure whatever you are building to a support beam in the ceiling or in the wall.

When you are using fabric in conjunction with a lamp or any type of electrical unit, always make sure you are using the fabric over a heat protective covering. For example, when doing a lampshade always adhere the fabric to the outside of the shade. Never use fabric where it can come into direct contact with heat. Always make sure you have a flameproof protection between fabric and heat source.

### Length and Width

Throughout the following pages constant reference is made to length and width. As you read, keep in mind that length always means the vertical measure and width always means the horizontal measure.

### Fabric

Most of the projects described are executed in lightweight and medium-weight fabric. This was done simply for ease of handling. The selection of fabric is really up to you. If you are not sure of a project, test-make it first with a lightweight fabric. When it works out to your satisfaction, remake the project in the fabric of your choice. This is a trick used by most designers and fine craftsmen.

When you are working with a 100 percent cotton fabric, remember to preshrink it—especially if the item you are making can be laundered and reused.

There really is no need to preshrink a cotton/polyester fabric. Also keep in mind that all new, unwashed fabrics have a sizing on them that acts as a protection against soot and dirt. New, unwashed fabrics are also usually brighter in color than laundered ones.

With each project I have allowed for a bit more fabric than is necessary; better to have too much than too little.

## Fusible Bonding Web

Fusible bonding web is used in numerous projects throughout this book. It is available in fabric stores, comes 18″ wide, is completely washable, and is fully dry-cleanable. Through a fusing action it joins fabrics together and becomes invisible when heat and steam from an iron are applied. The web is literally used in place of thread. Remember, however, that fabric that is fused together is not as strong as fabric that has been sewn together. Items you have fused must be treated and handled more gently than sewn items. Fusible bonding web needs lots of wet heat to make it work properly. I use a very damp washcloth to help in the fusing process and I always use two layers of the web wherever extra strength is needed. Follow the manufacturer's directions, but do experiment with the product just to make sure the directions are right for the project you are working on.

## Fusible Backing

Fusible backing is different from fusible bonding web in that it is not used between two pieces of material but is a stiff backing for one piece of fabric. It is available in fabric stores, comes 36″ wide, and is washable and dry-cleanable.

## Scissors or Fabric Shears?

Here is a very important piece of nickel knowledge you should store in your memory bank and remember every time you work with fabric and/or paper. Scissors are what one uses in school, at the office, in the kitchen, and so forth. The blades are usually thick and too dull to cut fabric without fraying it. Scissors are primarily used for cutting paper or anything other than fabric.

Fabric shears are sold in cutlery and sewing supply stores and should be used *only* to cut fabric. The blades should be razor sharp for all projects in this book so that when they cut, the fabric will not fray. They should never cut paper of any sort—not even tissue paper—for fear of dulling them. Because I own several pairs of fabric shears, I find that they must be sharpened frequently when I am working with a lot of polyester-blended fabrics. No doubt you will find the same to be true.

## Glue

White household glue is one of my favorites. It is easy to use (squeeze it right from the bottle if you wish), doesn't yellow when dry, and is water soluble. This last is very important to me because it means that I can glue, rip apart, change, and reglue quickly and easily.

Spray adhesive, the brother of brush-on rubber cement, is good to use if you want to do a gluing project in record time. Otherwise be careful. The adhesive tends to dry super fast and unless your aim is perfect, you may end up gluing more things than you had intended.

# SUPPLIES

If you are a nonsewer and/or new at doing how-to's, don't be confused by some of the items used throughout this book. They are all readily obtainable:

### Craft or Art Supply Store

Acrylic sealer
Heavy white cardboard
Mat knife
Pushpins
Rubber cement
Scissors
Stiff white paper
Spray adhesive
Stretcher bars
Foam-core board

### Fabric Store

Braid
Fabric shears
Fusible bonding web
Gimp
(an ornamental or flat braid)
Polyester batting
Polyester fleece padding
Rattail braid
Ribbon
T-pins

### Hardware Store

Brads (headless nails)
Nails
Paintbrush
Sponge paintbrush
Staple gun and staples
Vinyl-to-wall adhesive
White household glue
Wood glue
Wood joiners

## FABRIC WEIGHTS

### Lightweight

Batiste
Crinkle cotton
Gingham
Mosquito netting
Seersucker

### Medium-Weight

Chintz
Cotton chenille
Corduroy, pinwale
Moiré
Muslin
Percale
Piqué
Poplin
Pongee
Sheeting
Stretch terry
Toile

### Heavyweight

Brocade
Canvas
Corduroy, wide wale
Diving board matting
Felt
Sisal
Straw cloth
Ticking
Union cloth

# NO-SEW DECORATING

# DINETTE

Brightening a dinette area is easy when you cover an old or unpainted chest with fabric, create casement window curtains to add warmth to the area, and tie it all together by covering the walls . . . lighten the corner where you are!

## NO-SEW PROJECTS

*Casement Window Curtain*
*Covered Chest of Drawers*
*Fabric–Covered Walls—Pasted*

## CASEMENT WINDOW CURTAIN

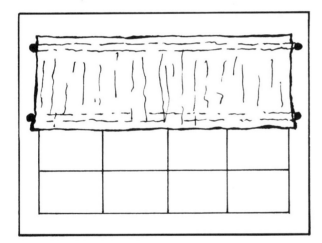

This is an easy way to conceal a bad view. The curtain can be made of inexpensive fabric and literally "tossed" when soiled.

### YOU NEED . . .

**Fabric**—lightweight, twice the width of curtain rod (tip to tip) + 1½" and once the length (distance from top of upper rod to bottom of lower rod) + 6"
**Tape measure**
**Marking pencil**

Fabric shears
Scissors
Fusible bonding web
Dressmaker's pins
Iron
2 café curtain rods and brackets or 2 sash curtain rods and brackets

### TO MAKE IT . . .

1.

CAFÉ RODS ATTACHED TO WINDOW FRAME AND SASH

Attach café or sash rods to window following manufacturer's directions. When installing them, remember to point top brackets up and bottom brackets down.

**2.**

RAW EDGE

¼″

FABRIC WRONG SIDE

½″

Press fabric flat. Trim off selvages.

Measure, mark, and cut out (use scissors because the bonding web will dull your fabric shears) two strips of fusible bonding web, each ¼″ wide and the length of your fabric panel. Turn raw side edges of panel under ¼″. Press, then fuse in place with bonding web following manufacturer's directions. Turn side edges under again ½″. Press and fuse in place with additional strips of bonding web cut to size.

**3.**

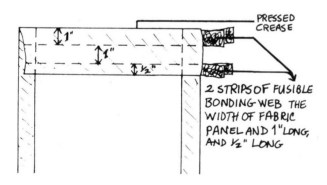

PRESSED CREASE

1″

1″

½″

2 STRIPS OF FUSIBLE BONDING WEB THE WIDTH OF FABRIC PANEL AND 1″ LONG, AND ½″ LONG

Turn down top of fabric panel 2½″ and press in place.

Measure, mark, and cut out (use scissors) two strips of fusible bonding web, each the width of the panel and 1″ long. Place bonding web between wrong sides of fabric along pressed crease, as illustrated.

Fuse heading in place following manufacturer's directions. Allow 1″ for casing (depending upon thickness of your rod, add or subtract with this measurement—casing should be a bit loose). Fuse hem into place with two strips

of bonding web, each the width of the fabric panel and ½″ long (if you end up with more than a ½″ hem, trim off the excess).

**4.** *Carefully* thread casing onto top curtain rod and place in top brackets. Gently arrange casement gathers. If you have the time, allow curtain to hang for a while then measure, mark, and pin-baste bottom heading, casing, and hem. Bottom measures should be equal to top measures.

Remove panel from rod and repeat fusing procedure for bottom of casement curtain.

**5.** *Carefully* thread top and bottom casings onto curtain rods. Place rods in their respective brackets. Gently arrange gathers.

# COVERED CHEST OF DRAWERS

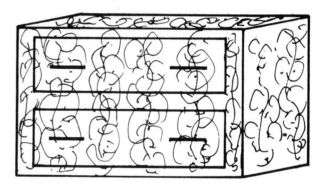

This is a beautiful way to glamorize a flea market purchase, unpainted, or old ugly furniture. This method works well when fabric has a definite repeat.

## YOU NEED . . .

**Chest of drawers**—painted flat white
**Fabric**—medium-weight. Amount needed depends upon the size of chest to be covered. You need enough to cover front, sides, and top of chest in one or two pieces of fabric with a 2″ turn under. (A sheet works nicely in this instance.)
**Tape measure**
**Marking pencil**

**Fabric shears**
**White household glue**
**Medium-size disposable container**
**Paintbrush**—2″ wide
**Steel ruler**
**Single-edge razor blade**
**Clear nail polish**
**Iron**

## TO MAKE IT . . .

**1.** Remove drawer handles from chest. Sand all rough edges.

**2.** Press fabric flat. Trim off selvages.

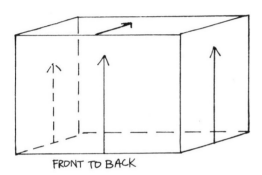

FRONT TO BACK

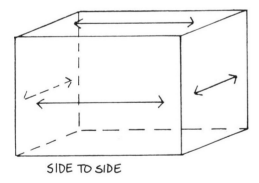

SIDE TO SIDE

If fabric you are using has a definite repeat, decide which way you want your fabric design to run—side to side, or front to back.

**3.** Treat chest of drawers as a giant package you are going to wrap; leave drawers in the chest.

**4.** Pour white household glue into disposable container and if necessary, dilute it with a tiny bit of water so that it spreads easily and evenly with a paintbrush.

**5.**

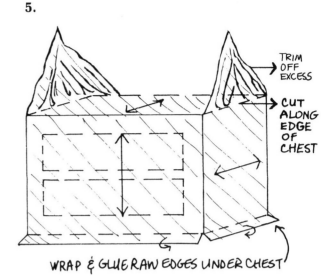

TRIM OFF EXCESS

CUT ALONG EDGE OF CHEST

WRAP & GLUE RAW EDGES UNDER CHEST

Brush an even coating of glue onto top of chest. Center fabric and smooth it into position making sure you have allowed enough fabric to cover the face of the chest plus 2″ extra for pattern alignment.
Brush glue onto face of chest and smooth fabric into position.

**6.** Brush glue onto sides and smooth fabric into place. Using fabric shears, cut away excess along top edges of chest. Wrap and glue raw edges of fabric to back and bottom of chest of drawers.
You now have a giant fabric-covered box.

**7.**

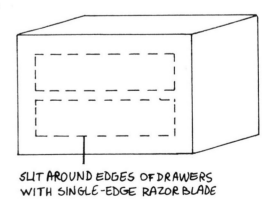

SLIT AROUND EDGES OF DRAWERS WITH SINGLE-EDGE RAZOR BLADE

Working with a single-edge razor blade and using a steel ruler as your guide, slit fabric around each drawer as illustrated. Tilt chest forward slightly to allow drawers to slide open.

Brush all raw fabric edges with clear nail polish to keep them from fraying when in use. Reattach drawer handles.

To protect the top of your covered chest of drawers cover it with a piece of glass cut to size.

# FABRIC-COVERED WALLS—PASTED

This is easy to do and easy to remove by saturating fabric with hot water and carefully peeling it off the wall. If you wish to reuse the fabric after removing it from the wall, first hand wash the adhesive out of it.

## YOU NEED . . .

**Walls**—clean white or off-white, and free of lumps, bumps, cracks, or crevices
**Fabric**—medium-weight, small all-over design, random print or stripe
**Chalk**
**String**—as long as wall is high + 12″
**Heavy weight**—to tie to end of string
**Tape measure**
**Marking pencil**
**Fabric shears**
**Premixed fabric-to-wall adhesive**
**Paintbrush**—3″ wide
**Steel ruler**

**Steel yardstick**
**Single-edge razor blades**
**Clear nail polish**
**Iron**

## TO MAKE IT . . .

**1.** To figure how much fabric you need measure height and width of area to be covered and add 2″ extra all around to allow for pattern alignment. If the fabric you are using has an obvious repeat, add one extra repeat in length to your requirements.

**2.** Press fabric flat. Trim off selvages. Measure, mark, and cut fabric into panels equal to the height of wall plus 4″. If you have doors or windows to contend with, cut smaller panels accordingly.

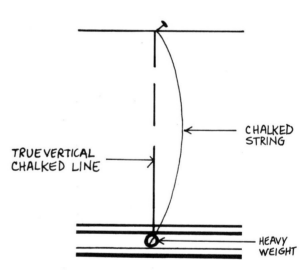

To establish the true vertical line of your wall for positioning fabric correctly, plumb line it. Thumbtack a piece of chalked string to the spot where the ceiling meets the wall and where you will paste your first length of fabric. Tie a heavy weight (rock, washer, hammer, etc.) to the end of the string near the floor to keep it taut. Hold the weight in place with one hand or foot and snap the chalked string with your other hand. If you have kept everything steady, the chalked line on the wall is the true vertical.

**3.**

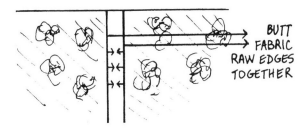

BUTT FABRIC RAW EDGES TOGETHER

Working from the top down, brush a light, even coating of premixed fabric-to-wall adhesive onto wall making sure the area you are covering is a bit wider than fabric panel. Allowing 2″ extra at top of wall, align fabric panel with plumb line and carefully smooth it into place with your hands. Do not pull or stretch the panel. If excess paste comes through the fabric, quickly wipe it off with a warm damp sponge. Repeat this procedure with each fabric panel, butting raw edges together and matching repeats until the entire wall area is covered.

**4.**

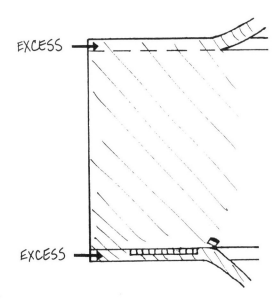

EXCESS

EXCESS

When fabric is semi-dry, trim away excess from top and bottom of wall using a single-edge razor blade and a steel ruler or yardstick as a guide. If fabric frays as you trim it, use a fresh razor blade. To hold straying threads in place coat all raw edges with clear nail polish.

For a more finished effect decorative molding can be nailed in place over the raw edges of the fabric—or use undiluted white household glue around the perimeter of the covered wall to attach ribbon or gimp.

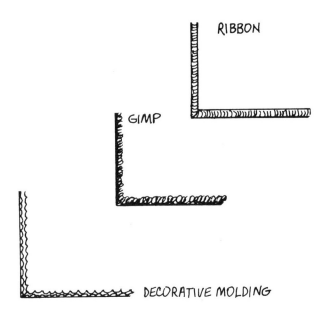

RIBBON

GIMP

DECORATIVE MOLDING

If you wish to fabric only a portion of the wall, top or bottom, follow the above directions and stop wherever you wish. Generally chair rail or wainscoting level is a good guide (3 to 4 feet above the floor). The raw edges can be easily hidden with half-round molding or covered lattice stripping. This is also an effective way to piece a length of fabric together.

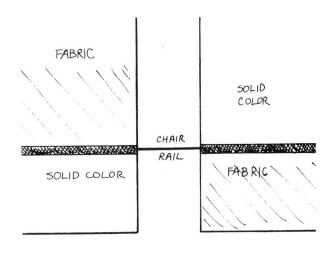

FABRIC

SOLID COLOR

CHAIR RAIL

SOLID COLOR

FABRIC

# DINING ROOM

This dining room situation offers sophistication, comfort, and easy decorating all rolled into one. A festoon compliments the window, and plain chandelier shades can be covered and changed at a moment's notice.

## NO-SEW PROJECTS

*Covered Slip Seat*
*Festoon (or Swag)*
*Napkins*
*Covered Plain Paper Lampshade*
*Square Floor-Length Table Skirt*
*Square Overskirt for a Square Table*

## COVERED SLIP SEAT

Many side chairs have an upholstered wooden seat that slips out of its framework allowing for easy recovering.

### YOU NEED . . .

For covering four slip seats, each approximately 19½″ × 16″ × 15½″:
**Fabric**—medium- to heavyweight, 1 yard 54″ wide
**Tape measure**
**Marking pencil**
**Fabric shears**
**Staple gun and staples**
**Iron**

### TO MAKE IT . . .

**1.** To cover one seat, turn chair upside down and remove all corner screws. Although new fabric really should not be placed on top of

old, on some slip seats the old fabric is all that is holding the padding in place. If chair seat has a muslin covering underneath, remove old fabric. If it does not, leave well enough alone and put new fabric on top of the old.

**2.**

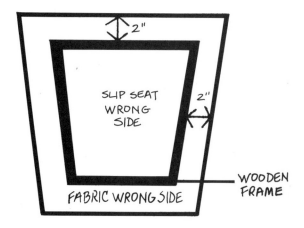

Press fabric flat. Trim off selvages.
Place fabric, wrong side up, on a smooth flat

surface. Place chair seat, upside down, on top of fabric. If fabric has a design, position seat to its best advantage. Measure, mark, and cut out fabric around slip seat so that it is 2" larger than seat on all sides. Flip seat and fabric together to right side up to make sure fabric is properly aligned. Return to wrong side up position.

3.

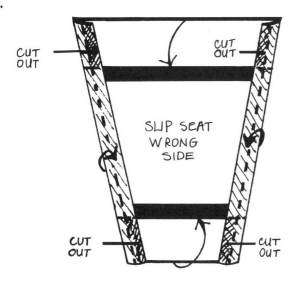

Tautly wrap and staple fabric along two opposite sides of slip seat. Trim away excess and cut out fabric from corners as illustrated to eliminate bulk. Tautly wrap and staple fabric along front and back sides. Make sure corners are neat and even. Trim away excess fabric. Return slip seat to chair framework and secure in position.

# FESTOON (OR SWAG)

This is a beautiful way to enhance a window with a view. No plants, draperies, or curtains to get in the way and just enough fabric to add warmth to the area.

## *YOU NEED* . . .

**Fabric**—any weight, must be ½ times wider than window frame's outer edges and 1½ to 2 times the length of the area you wish to cover

**Tape measure**
**Marking pencil**
**Fabric shears**
**Pushpins**
**Staple gun and staples**
**Double-faced carpet tape**
**Iron**
**Trim**—self-fabric strips or ribbon cut into pieces half the length of the window
**Optional**—wood lattice stripping cut to size to fit around upper quarter of window frame
**Saw**
**Hammer**
**Finishing nails** (headless nails)

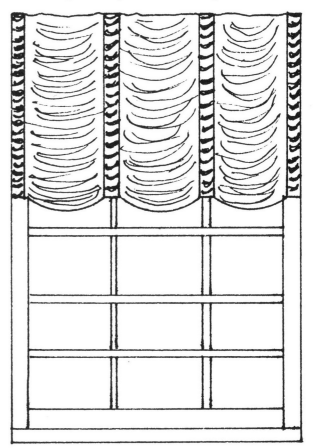

## TO MAKE IT . . .

Before you attach your fabric you might want to install lattice stripping around the upper quarter of the window frame and use that as a stapling base. Nail stripping across top width of window (or top width of window at ceiling level) and down sides as far as you wish to go. One-quarter the way down is usually more than sufficient.

**1.** Press fabric flat. If you are using the entire width of the fabric, leave selvages on. If you cut into the width at all, make sure you remove selvages so that "give" of fabric will be consistent on both sides.

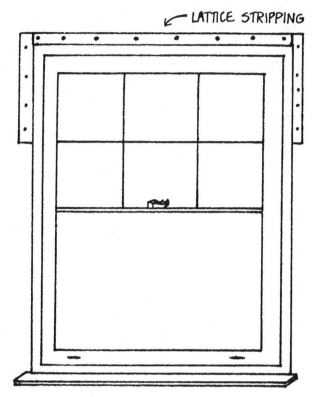

LATTICE STRIPPING

**2.** Measure, mark, and cut out a section of fabric one-half again wider than width of window and 1½ to 2 times the length of top quarter of window—a bit longer if you are extending the fabric beyond window frame onto lattice stripping. If you wish a reversible festoon, double your fabric requirements and work two pieces together, right sides out. Turn top raw edges in 1½" and press in place.

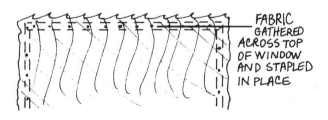

FABRIC GATHERED ACROSS TOP OF WINDOW AND STAPLED IN PLACE

**3.** Staple top side edges of fabric to each side of window frame or onto lattice stripping. Ease fabric into a gathered effect across top of window. It will look all crumpled—it's supposed to.

**4.**

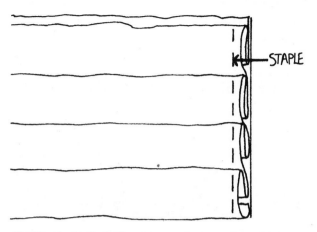

STAPLE

FABRIC PLEATED AND STAPLED TO SIDE OF WINDOW

Now pleat fabric (as you would a skirt) down each side, use pushpins to hold in place, then staple them in position on opposite sides of window. Make pleats as deep as you wish. Try to use up the entire length of fabric. If you feel the festoon has too heavy an appearance using all the fabric, trim some off and make your pleats more shallow.

**5.**

STRIPS TAPED IN PLACE

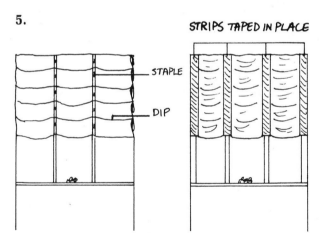

STAPLE

DIP

Depending upon the width of your window and the number of panes in the upper half, measure and mark where you would like the festoon to dip. Use pushpin, then staple along frames of panes to hold fabric in place. Measure, mark, and cut out enough fabric strips to cover each vertical line of staples 1¼" wide and as long as the festoon plus 2". Turn raw edges under ¼" on each side and press in place. Attach strips to staple heads with double-faced carpet tape.

If your window has no panes, create dips by stapling strips of ribbon or fabric with edges turned under at top of window, room side in. Run strips down room side of festoon, under and up window side. Pull strips up to achieve desired fullness of dip and secure in place by stapling them to window frame. Give each pleat a little tug to create the dip.

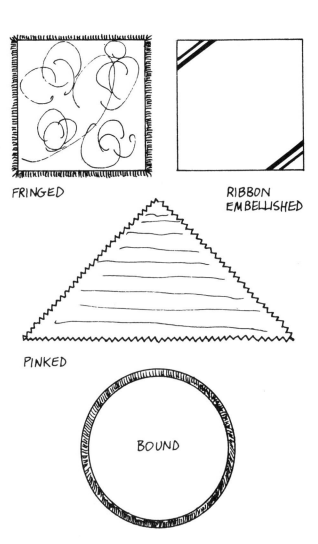

FRINGED

RIBBON EMBELLISHED

PINKED

BOUND

# NAPKINS

Napkins are a wonderful way to use up scraps of fabric from a no-sew project. They can be made in almost any size and shape you wish and, as you know, cloth napkins always add a touch of refinement to any festive occasion.

My personal rule of thumb for napkin sizes is as follows:

### Dining Napkins
Breakfast—16″ to 20″
Luncheon—18″ to 20″
Dinner—20″ to 22″

### Cocktail Napkins
Square—7½″ × 7½″
Rectangular—6″ × 8″

### Tea Napkins
Square—10″ × 10″

No-sew napkins can be pinked, fringed, or embellished with washable ribbons secured in place with fusible bonding web.

 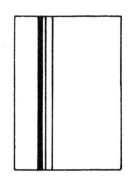

RIBBON EMBELLISHED

# COVERED PLAIN PAPER LAMPSHADE

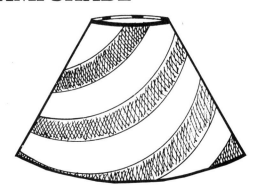

These directions apply to any size plain paper lampshade. Make sure the shade you are covering is smooth and white or off-white so that it will not change the color of the fabric you are working with.

## YOU NEED . . .

**Plain paper lampshade**
**Fabric**—light- to medium-weight. Paper pattern will determine how much you need.
**Sheets of newspaper**—enough to wrap around lampshade
**Cellophane tape**
**Scissors**
**Fabric shears**
**Dressmaker's pins**
**Marking pencil**
**White household glue**
**Small disposable container**
**Paintbrush**—1½″ wide
**Paper adhesive with applicator**
**Iron**
**Optional trim**—narrow braid or ribbon

## TO MAKE IT . . .

1.

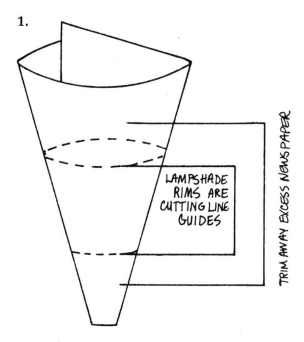

The size of your shade will determine whether or not you tape two sheets of newspaper together to create one large one. Wrap newspaper around lampshade in a funnel-like fashion, making sure the shade is completely covered. Use a piece of tape to keep paper in wrapped position. Holding wrapped shade in one hand and using rims as cutting guides, trim away excess paper from top and bottom of shade.

2.

Remove newly created paper pattern from shade. Trim sides of pattern down so that you have a 1″ overlap when it is rewrapped around shade.

3.

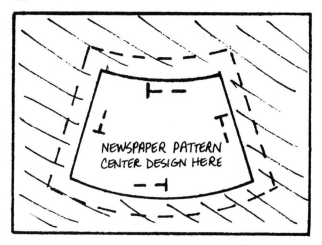

Press fabric flat. Trim off selvages.
Carefully center paper pattern on top of right side of fabric to show off motif to its best advantage. Pin pattern in place. Measure, mark, and cut out fabric ½″ larger on all sides than paper pattern.

**4.** Pour white household glue into disposable container and, if necessary, dilute with a tiny bit of water so that it spreads easily and evenly with a paintbrush.

**5.** Carefully brush an even coating of glue onto lampshade. Beginning at the seam, wrap fabric, right side out, around shade and smooth it into place allowing ½″ to overlap top rim and ½″ to overlap bottom rim. Trim raw edges at seam to overlap ⅛″.

**6.** Allow shade to dry. Trim fabric overlaps down to be equal with paper overlaps on inside of shade.

**7.**

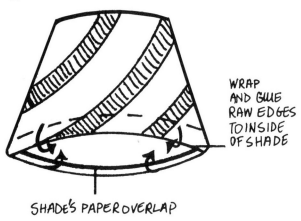

WRAP AND GLUE RAW EDGES TO INSIDE OF SHADE

SHADE'S PAPER OVERLAP

cutting out a square, the measure will be the same for the length.

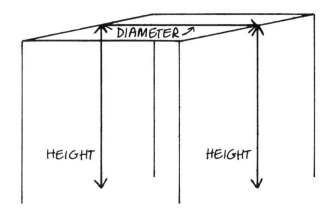

DIAMETER

HEIGHT          HEIGHT

Brush a thin coating of paper adhesive around top and bottom rims of shade. Allow adhesive to become tacky. Wrap raw edges of fabric around rims to inside of shade and notch if necessary to avoid puckering. Hold fabric in place for a few minutes until glue "sets." Allow to dry thoroughly.

**8.** Leave shade untrimmed, or trim as you desire with braid or ribbon.

## SQUARE OVERSKIRT FOR A SQUARE TABLE

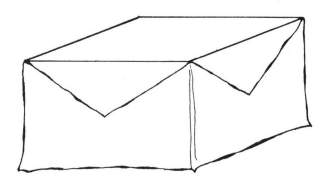

## SQUARE FLOOR-LENGTH TABLE SKIRT

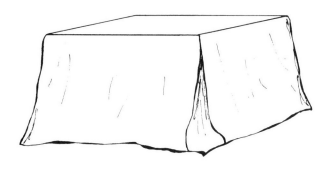

To make a square floor-length table skirt, measure your table as follows: height + diameter + height. This will tell you how wide your fabric must be. Because you are

I cut my overskirts "by eye." Beginning with the same size square as your undercloth (or one a bit smaller) and using pinking shears, keep trimming the overskirt down equally on all four sides until you arrive at the size you think is most attractive over your square floor-length table skirt.

If you are a bit unsure about using my "by eye" method, the following hypothetical cutting guide for a floor-length card table undercloth and overskirt will help you. (Card tables come in many different sizes. Therefore, measure your own table carefully before cutting into your fabric.) Use illustrations as guides only—not as "law."

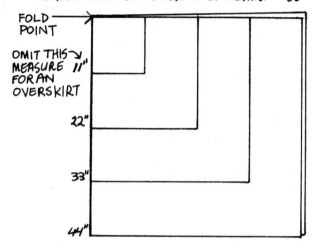

FINISHED SIZE OF SQUARE TABLE SKIRT — 88"

FOLD POINT

OMIT THIS MEASURE 11" FOR AN OVERSKIRT

22"

33"

44"

If you need overskirts for an 88" square floor-length table skirt, you begin with an 88" square of fabric folded into quarters. You now have a 44" folded square. Divide 44" into quarters (11", 22", 33", 44") as illustrated. The 11" square is not worth cutting for an overskirt, but the 22" and 33" squares are good cutting guides to follow (33" is a bit large so cut it down a bit). From these measures you can increase or decrease the size of your over-skirts. Remember to measure carefully before you begin cutting and also remember that only one overskirt can be cut from a folded fabric square. For each overskirt you must fold a separate square of fabric into the dimensions you desire. No matter what size your finished cloth is, the principle of quarters will work. If your overskirt is larger than 72" square, use a sheet—widths go up to 102".

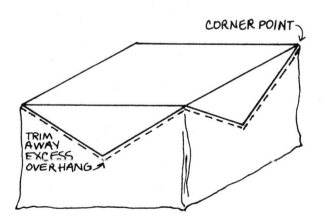

CORNER POINT

TRIM AWAY EXCESS OVERHANG

Place overskirt on top of undercloth. Using pinking shears, carefully trim the points of overskirt so that excess corner overhang is trimmed away and tapered into each corner as illustrated. Do not expose the table's corner points.

If you wish to create a hemmed effect on the overskirt, don't trim it down as much. Turn raw edges under and secure them in place with fusible bonding web following manufacturer's directions.

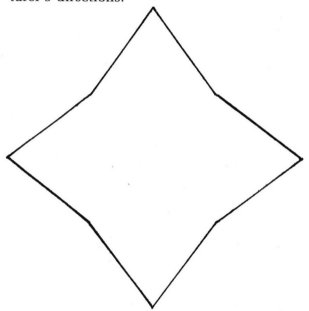

TRIMMED OVERSKIRT

# POWDER ROOM

A powder room is usually the smallest room you will ever decorate. Therefore, make the room look important. With fabric shutters and fabric-covered walls you can easily make every inch count.

## NO-SEW PROJECTS

*Fabric Shutters*
*Padded Mirror Frame*
*Radiator Cover*
*Fabric-Covered Walls—Liquid Starched*

## FABRIC SHUTTERS

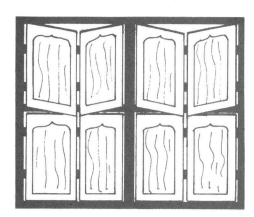

These are a quick way to spruce up a room. I like them because they can literally be disposed of each season without regrets. Little labor and little fabric have been used.

### YOU NEED . . .

**Fabric shutter frames**—purchased at local lumberyard and installed at window following manufacturer's directions
**Fabric**—light- or medium-weight. For each panel, 1½ times the width of casement rod, tip to tip, and once the length (distance from top of upper rod to bottom of lower rod) + 1".
**Tape measure**
**Marking pencil**
**Fabric shears**
**Scissors**
**Pinking shears**
**Fusible bonding web**
**Iron**

### TO MAKE IT . . .

1.

Install fabric shutters at window following manufacturer's directions.

**2.** Press fabric flat. Trim off selvages.
For each shutter fabric panel measure, mark, and use pinking shears to cut out a section of fabric 1½ times the width of the casement rod, tip to tip, and once the length (distance from top of upper rod to bottom of lower rod) plus 1″.

**3.** Measure, mark, and cut out (use scissors, the bonding web will dull your fabric shears) four strips of fusible bonding web the width of your fabric panel and ¼″ long.

**4.**

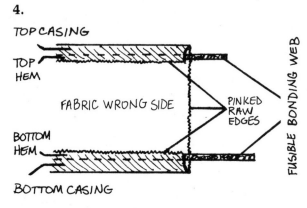

Turn top and bottom edges of fabric panel under ½″ inch and press in place. Place two strips of bonding web along wrong side of pinked raw edges and fuse wrong sides of panel together following manufacturer's directions to form a casing along top and bottom.

**5.** *Carefully* thread fabric panel onto top and bottom rods of shutter frame (the casings will fit tightly). Place rods in their respective holes and gently adjust gathers making sure that pinked side edges do not show on right side of shutter.

# PADDED MIRROR FRAME

This is an attractive way to add a sophisticated softness to bare walls. Select fabric that is already part of your room decor or else make sure it is distinctive in its own right and complements your other accessories.

## YOU NEED . . .

**Wooden picture frame** (rectangle or square) or frame made out of artist's stretcher bars or frame made out of plywood—cut to size
**Fabric**—medium-weight, cut to twice the size of frame
**Polyester batting**—cut to twice the size of frame
**Wood stripping**—¼″ thick and as wide as depth of frame to fit around inside rim of frame
**Tape measure**
**Fabric shears**
**Brads** (headless nails)—¾″ long
**Hammer**
**White household glue**
**Small disposable container**
**Paintbrush**—½″ wide
**Staple gun and staples**
**Grosgrain ribbon**—to trim around inside rim of frame; one, two, or three colors and widths no wider than depth of frame
**Iron**

## TO MAKE IT . . .

**1.** Press fabric flat. Trim off selvages.

**2.**

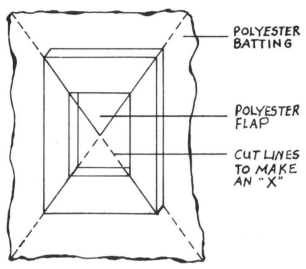

POLYESTER BATTING

POLYESTER FLAP

CUT LINES TO MAKE AN "X"

**3.**

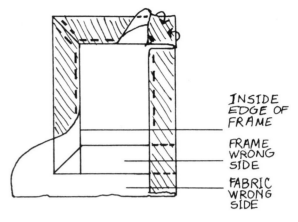

INSIDE EDGE OF FRAME

FRAME WRONG SIDE

FABRIC WRONG SIDE

Working with wrong side up, place padded frame on top of fabric. Measure, mark, and cut out a section of fabric large enough so that it wraps smoothly to the inside edge of frame. Staple in place. Miter corners.

**4.**

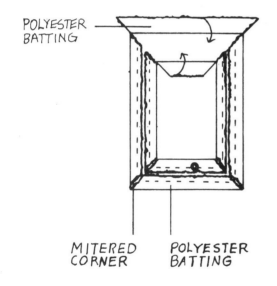

POLYESTER BATTING

MITERED CORNER

POLYESTER BATTING

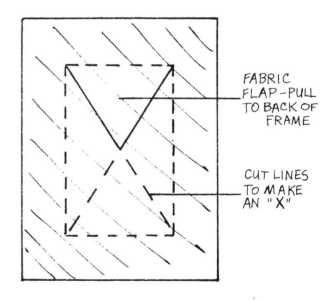

FABRIC FLAP - PULL TO BACK OF FRAME

CUT LINES TO MAKE AN "X"

Place polyester batting on top of frame, which is right side up. Loosely wrap batting around frame and staple to back along center of wood. Flip frame to right side up and cut an X in the center of batting, going into each corner. Pull batting flaps to back of frame, and trim away all excess so that raw edges of batting meet—but do not overlap. Staple in place along center back of wood. Miter each corner.

Flip frame to right side up. Mark and carefully cut a large X in the center of inside edges of frame, going well into each corner. Pull flaps to back of frame (don't pull too tautly or you will lose the rounded effect of the batting), trim away excess fabric, and staple in place along back of frame. Don't worry if your fabric flaps expose some of the batting in the corners, it will be covered later.

**5.**

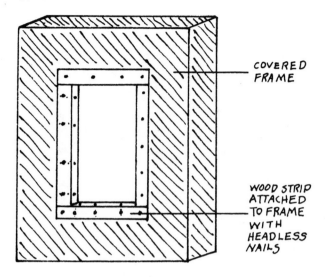

COVERED FRAME

WOOD STRIP ATTACHED TO FRAME WITH HEADLESS NAILS

Attach wood strips to inside edges of frame with headless nails.

**6.**

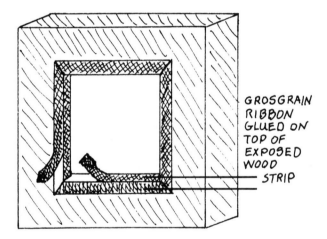

GROSGRAIN RIBBON GLUED ON TOP OF EXPOSED WOOD STRIP

Pour white household glue into small disposable container. Do not dilute it. Working with frame right side up, brush glue onto exposed sides of wood strips in a thin, even layer. Allow glue to become a bit tacky. Beginning and ending in a corner, glue ribbon into place around inside rim of frame, covering all exposed wood strips. Miter corners where necessary.

**7.** Take padded frame to your local mirror and glass cutter and have mirror and cardboard cut and installed to fit onto back of frame. He will usually attach wire for hanging as well.

# RADIATOR COVER

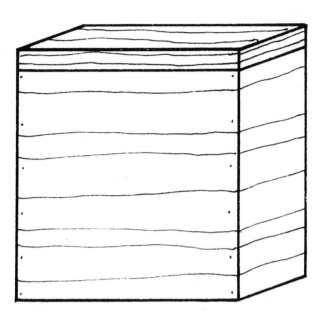

This is an attractive and economical way to hide an old radiator. Just remember that after a winter's use, the fabric will be soiled and should be changed to keep its fresh appearance. Therefore, don't cut just one, cut two covers and store the extra one in preparation for next season.

## YOU NEED . . .

**12 artist's stretcher bars**—6 height of radiator or a bit more, 4 width of sides, 2 width of front
**Plywood**—½" thick, cut to size for top
**Fabric**—medium-weight. Amount needed depends upon the size of the radiator cover you are making. You need enough to cover front sides and top plus 18" extra for turn unders on stretcher bars.
**Tape measure**
**Marking pencil**
**Fabric shears**
**Pushpins**
**Staple gun and staples**
**Finishing nails** (headless nails)
**Hammer**
**Iron**

# TO MAKE IT...

**1.**

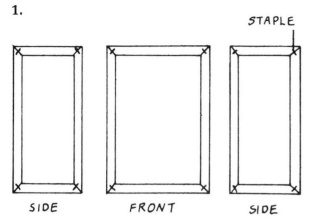

SIDE     FRONT     SIDE

Push stretcher bars together to form three frames: two for sides of radiator cover and one for the front. Staple each corner as illustrated to keep frames stable.

If fabric you are using has a light-colored background, paint stretcher bar frames flat white before continuing this project. If the frame still shows through fabric, back all pieces of fabric with white batiste.

**2.** To cover each stretcher bar frame, measure, mark, and cut out a piece of fabric 4″ longer and wider than frame.

**3.**

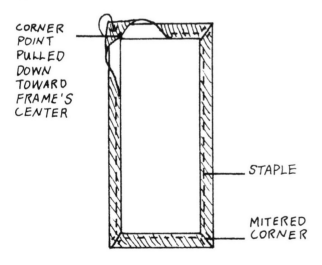

CORNER POINT PULLED DOWN TOWARD FRAME'S CENTER

STAPLE

MITERED CORNER

Center fabric, right side up, on top of frame. Use pushpins to hold it in place. Wrap fabric around to back and staple in place beginning at the center of each side and working out toward corners. To do corners pull corner

point of fabric down toward frame's center and staple to hold in place. Fold remaining excess fabric over to form a mitered corner. Remove pushpins.

**4.**

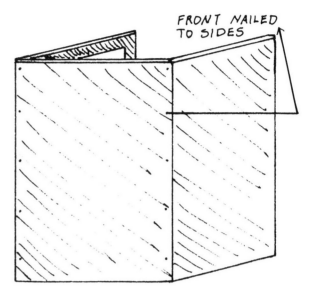

FRONT NAILED TO SIDES

Place covered side frames at right angles to covered front frame and join together with finishing nails—well-spaced (if fabric is a loose weave, push nails through fabric so that they disappear). Small angle irons and screws will also work.

**5.** Make sure plywood top fits flush with all sides when placed on top of covered radiator sides.

Measure, mark, and cut out a section of fabric 4″ longer and wider than plywood top. Wrap and staple fabric around top as previously explained in step #3. Place covered top on top of covered radiator frame.

# FABRIC-COVERED WALLS—LIQUID STARCHED

This method is messy, but probably one of the easiest and most economical to do and the fastest to remove. Simply peel it off. If you wish to reuse the fabric, machine wash starch out of it first.

## YOU NEED . . .

**Walls**—clean white or off-white, and free of lumps, bumps, cracks, or crevices
**Fabric**—small all-over design, random print or stripe, medium-weight
**Chalk**
**String**—as long as wall is high + 12″
**Heavy weight**—to tie to end of string
**Tape measure**
**Marking pencil**
**Fabric shears**
**Pushpins**
**Large pan or basin**
**Liquid starch**
**Large sponge**
**Steel ruler**
**Steel yardstick**
**Single-edge razor blades**
**Plastic tarp sheets**
**Iron**

## TO MAKE IT . . .

**1.** To figure how much fabric you need measure height and width of area to be covered and add 2″ extra all around to allow for pattern alignment. If fabric you are using has an obvious repeat, add one extra repeat in length to your requirements.

**2.** Press fabric flat. Trim off selvages. Measure, mark, and cut fabric into panels equal to height of wall plus 4″. If you have doors or windows to deal with, cut panels accordingly.

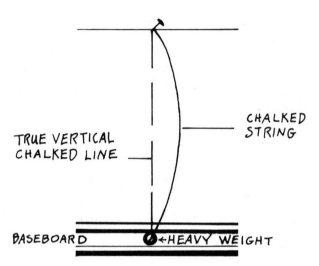

To establish the true vertical line of your wall for positioning fabric correctly, plumb line it. Thumbtack a piece of chalked string to the spot where the ceiling meets the wall and where you will paste your first length of fabric. Tie a heavy weight (rock, washer, hammer, etc.) to the end of the string near the floor to keep it taut. Hold the weight in place with one hand or foot and snap the chalked string with your other hand. If you have kept everything steady, the chalked line on the wall is the true vertical.

**3.** Cover floor with plastic tarp sheets to protect it (liquid starch removes varnish).

**4.** Pour starch into a large pan or basin. Soak sponge in it.
Beginning at the top, liberally smear starch over wall making sure the area you are covering is a bit wider than fabric panel.

**5.**

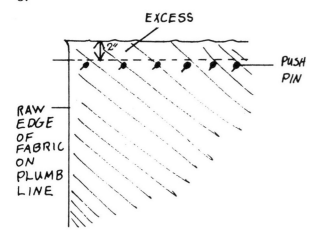

Allowing 2″ extra at top of wall, align fabric panel with plumb line and carefully smooth it into place with your hands. Place pushpins across top of fabric panel to hold it in place while you work. If area you previously starched dries, apply more to keep it wet as you smooth fabric into position working your way down the wall.

Now liberally coat face of fabric with a layer of liquid starch, making sure it is soaked through. Repeat these procedures with each fabric panel, butting raw edges together and matching repeats as you do so until the entire wall area is covered.

**6.**

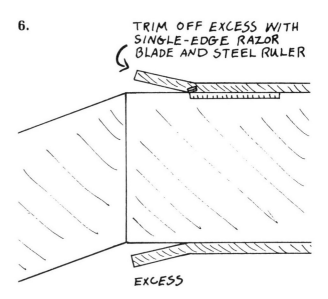

When fabric is dry, trim away excess from top and bottom of wall using a single-edge razor blade and steel ruler or yardstick as a guide. If fabric frays as you trim it, use a fresh razor blade.

# DEN

A den or study can afford the luxury of deep drama . . . so why not do it! A den isn't always large so make the most of the space you have and create a strong decorating statement with rich, deep colors.

## NO-SEW PROJECTS

*Covered Parsons Table*
*Covered Venetian Blind*
*Walls—Fabri-Trak® System*

## COVERED PARSONS TABLE

The design of this table originated at, and was named for, the Parsons School of Design. The design of this table has been so overwhelmingly popular through the years that it is now available in many sizes and materials. Wood and plastic Parsons tables offer an excellent base for many types of coverings . . . fabric, leather, suedelike fabric, mirror, tile, rope, shell, bamboo, and so forth.

If the table you are working on is a color, paint it flat white before you begin this project so that it will not tint the fabric.

*YOU NEED . . .*

**Parsons table**—16″ plastic

**Fabric**—medium- to heavyweight, 54″ wide, without a definite repeat
**Tape measure**
**Marking pencil**
**Fabric shears**
**White household glue**
**Small disposable container**
**Paintbrush**—2″ wide
**Iron**

## TO MAKE IT . . .

1.

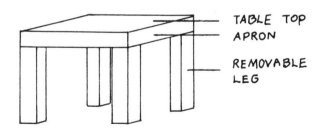

TABLE TOP
APRON
REMOVABLE LEG

Press fabric flat. Trim off selvages.
Measure, mark, and cut out a square of fabric

to equal the size of tabletop plus aprons (sides) plus 4″—approximately 24″ × 24″. If fabric has a design, position square to its best advantage. Be careful not to take away from the fabric you need for covering the legs.

**2.** Pour white household glue into disposable container and, if necessary, dilute it with a tiny bit of water so that glue spreads easily and evenly with a paintbrush.

**3.**
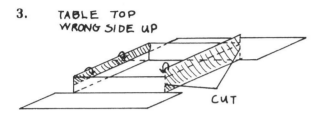
TABLE TOP WRONG SIDE UP

CUT

Brush an even coating of glue onto tabletop. Center fabric and smooth it into position. Flip top wrong side up. Glue two opposite sides into place and cut fabric at each corner as illustrated. Brush glue onto underside of aprons and glue raw edges of fabric into place.

**4.**
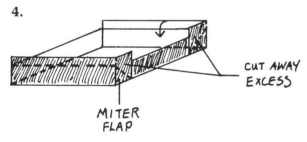
CUT AWAY EXCESS

MITER FLAP

Glue two remaining sides to aprons and cut on dotted lines as indicated to achieve a mitered corner. Glue miter flaps in place.

**5.** To cover legs, measure, mark, and cut out four rectangles, each equal to the leg circumference plus ½″ overlap and the leg height plus 1″ overlap.

**6.**
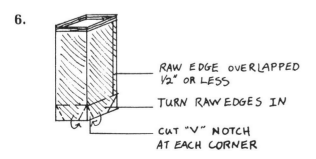
RAW EDGE OVERLAPPED ½″ OR LESS

TURN RAW EDGES IN

CUT "V" NOTCH AT EACH CORNER

Working with one leg at a time, brush glue onto all four sides. Beginning at a corner and in ridge at top of leg, wrap fabric around leg, smoothing it as you do so. Overlap raw edges ½″ or less. (If legs cannot be removed from tabletop, begin fabric on leg where apron stops.)
Notch each corner of excess fabric at bottom of leg. Brush inside of leg with glue and turn raw edges in. Repeat procedure for remaining legs. Allow all to dry thoroughly, then carefully push legs into tabletop. To protect tabletop, cover it with a square of glass cut to size.

# COVERED VENETIAN BLIND

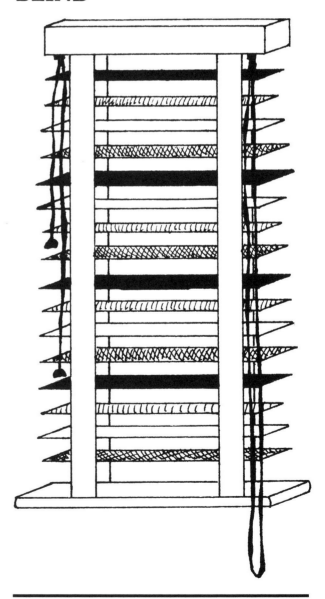

Venetian blinds were first introduced from the East to Venice by Marco Polo, and are one of the most effective ways presently known to control light at a window.

Covering a venetian blind isn't fast—just easy. It's an excellent way to give a color-filled "face lift" to a window and the blind's white metal or painted wooden slats. Covering the slats with fabric doesn't harm the blind at all. White household glue is used, which is water soluble. The fabric can be removed at any time from a metal venetian blind by soaking it in a tub of warm soapy water. To remove fabric from a wooden venetian blind, saturate fabric with a warm water-filled sponge. Sponge off glue residue.

## YOU NEED . . .

**Metal venetian blind**
**Fabric**—light- to medium-weight, solid color. Number and width of slats will determine how much you need.
**Fabric shears**
**Marking pencil**
**Tape measure**
**White household glue**
**Small disposable container**
**Paintbrush**—1½″ wide
**Manicure scissors**
**Clear nail polish**
**Double-faced carpet tape**
**Iron**

## TO MAKE IT . . .

**1.** Remove venetian blind from window brackets and wash it in a bath of warm soapy water. Rinse it thoroughly and allow blind to dry completely before beginning this project.

**2.**

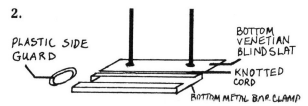

PLASTIC SIDE GUARD
BOTTOM VENETIAN BLIND SLAT
KNOTTED CORD
BOTTOM METAL BAR CLAMP

Remove bottom metal bar clamp and plastic side guards from bottom blind slat and unknot

the cords on each side. Pull cords to top of venetian blind, releasing each slat as you do so. Sliding it out sideways, remove each slat from its twill or plastic ladder tape.

**3.** The directions below are for covering a metal venetian blind. (To cover a wooden venetian blind follow all steps in these directions and adapt where necessary, that is, sponge blind clean; do not soak it in hot soapy water.)

To figure how much fabric you need to cover your venetian blind, measure each slat's width + ½″ and its depth × 2 + ½″, multiplied by the number of slats you must cover. Allow ¼ yard additional fabric for covering top trough of blind and bottom slat casing.

**4.** Press fabric flat. Trim off selvages.

**5.**

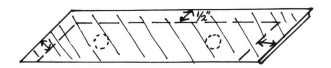

To cover one slat, measure, mark, and cut out a section of fabric large enough to wrap around front and back of slat and ½″ larger than slat on three sides. Continue measuring, marking, and cutting out enough single layers of fabric to cover every slat of the venetian blind. If you are using several solid colors, cut enough of each so that you can experiment and create a complementing color arrangement for your window.

**6.** Pour white household glue into disposable container and, if necessary, dilute it with a tiny bit of water so that glue spreads easily and evenly with a paintbrush.

**7.** Working with one slat at a time, brush a light, even coating of glue onto front and back of slat. The glue will form tiny beads. Allow glue beads to become a bit tacky. Wrap fabric section, right side out, around slat. Make sure glue does not come through the fabric. If it does, it will spot. Practice until you know exactly how much glue to brush onto each slat without having it show through. Follow same procedure to cover all slats. Cover bottom slat casing with a section of fabric in the same manner as you did the slats and push raw edges to the inside. Allow all to dry thoroughly.

**8.**

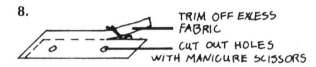

TRIM OFF EXCESS FABRIC

CUT OUT HOLES WITH MANICURE SCISSORS

Trim off excess fabric. Use manicure scissors to cut out holes for cording to pass through. Brush all raw edges with a light coating of clear nail polish.

**9.** To reassemble blind, you might want a friend to help you. Return covered slats to their ladder tape shelves and rethread with cords. (If the cording is nylon, burn the tips with a match so that the ends will not fray when they are dropped through the holes of the slats.) Hold the venetian blind up with one hand and straighten the slats so that they are perfectly even and flat. Make sure the different colors are where you want them. Knot the ends of the cords. Slide covered casing over the bottom slat and push on plastic side guards. If the metal trough at the top of the venetian blind is offensive to you, cover it, being careful to push the fabric well into each groove.

**10.**

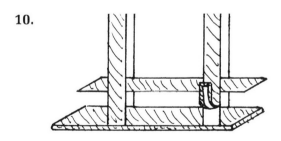

Rehang venetian blind in window. If the twill or plastic ladder tape is not compatible with the covered slats, measure, mark, and cut out four strips of fabric (ribbon may also be used) ¼″ larger on all sides than the length and width of the tapes. Turn raw edges under ¼″ on each side and press. Attach strips to ladder tape with double-faced carpet tape.

# WALLS—FABRI-TRAK® SYSTEM

An alternative to pasting, stapling, shirring, or upholstering a wall is to use the Fabri-Trak System. Fabri-Trak is a patented frame of fireproof ridged vinyl which is attached to the perimeter of a wall with screws, nails, or silicone live rubber cement, or any other appropriate bonding agent. It can be installed over plaster, sheet rock, concrete block, tile, or wood surfaces.

The face side of the Fabri-Trak has a strong adhesive surface with a finger lift tape to aid in one-person installation. With no advance surface preparation, the fabric is roughly cut to dimension and placed over the framework, held in position by the adhesive surface.

The rough cut excess or remaining tail (approximately 1″ extra all around) of the fabric is then inserted through a specially designed expandable and contractable hidden inlet jaw (with the help of a patented tool, "Sammy Stuffer" which is purchased along with the Fabri-Trak) and nests in a storage channel, leaving a perfectly crisp clean edge and a beautiful fabric wall surface.

When you want to remove fabric from the wall, begin in a corner and place "Sammy Stuffer" back into the trak. Pivot it slightly and pry track open. Place a piece of emery cloth or an emery board with its abrasive side facing you into the trak. Remove "Sammy Stuffer," then remove the emery. When this comes out the 1″ border will come out, then the rest of the fabric will follow. An entire wall can be undone in a few fast minutes enabling you to replace it instantly with a fresh new pattern. Fabri-Trak is sold in major department stores throughout America. For exact locations and availability write to Fabri-Trak, 681 Main Street, Building 30, Belleville, New Jersey 07109.

# PORCH

*The nice thing about decorating a porch is that you will probably want to rearrange and redecorate it every season . . . do so! You can give the room a whole new look in just a few short hours.*

## NO-SEW PROJECTS

**Floor-to-Ceiling Padded Folding Screen**
**Game Tabletop—Backgammon**
**Game Tabletop—Checkers**
**Shirred Folding Screen**

## FLOOR-TO-CEILING PADDED FOLDING SCREEN

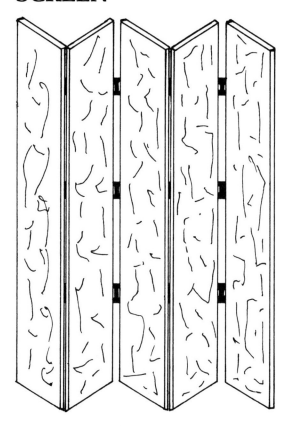

This is an ideal way to hide an ugly view or create an instant storage area. I like to use

covered screens in areas where there is a door next to a large picture window covered with draperies. In a living room a floor-to-ceiling screen can be covered in the same fabric as the draperies or the wall, to add architectural interest to an otherwise dull corner, and it can be easily moved. When the door is not in use, the screen becomes an integral part of your decorating scheme.

Folding screens, in any size, can be made of stretcher bars, 1″ × 2″ pine, or hollow doors. They are usually joined in increments of three, five, or seven panels. Stretcher bar screens are excellent for hiding radiators or open fireplace cavities during the summer months. Stretcher bars range in length from approximately 6″ to 60″ and are easily pushed together to create rectangles or squares. Pine, 1″ × 2″, is cut to size and can be assembled into screen frames at your local lumberyard. Doors, of course, are a ready-made source for screens. Remember, when joining the screen panels together always use bifold hinges— these allow for more mobility in the completed project.

## YOU NEED . . .

**1″ × 2″ pine frames**—no smaller than 12″ wide and as tall as the height of your wall (If you are not into "building," your local lumberyard can easily make screen panels to your specifications.)
**Plywood**—¼″ thick
**Metal wood joiners**
**Hammer**
**Saw**
**Square**
**Wood glue**
**Brads** (headless nails)—¾″ long
**Sandpaper**—medium grid
**Fabric**—length and width of each panel + 1″ extra all around
**Polyester batting**—length and width of each panel
**Tape measure**
**Marking pencil**
**Fabric shears**
**Scissors**
**Pushpins**
**Staple gun and staples**
**Bifold hinges**—quantity depends upon the height of screen. Ask your lumberyard.
**White household glue**
**Optional trim**—ribbon, width of panel's sides and enough to go around each panel

## TO MAKE IT . . .

Have your local lumberyard construct screen panels for you, or make them yourself as follows:

**1.** To make one panel, measure, mark, and cut two pieces of 1″ × 2″ pine the height you desire and four pieces the width you desire.

**2.** Make a panel by joining the two long side pieces of wood to the two short pieces, as illustrated. Make sure the 1″ side of wood faces up. Use metal wood joiners and glue to hold the pieces together and attach four interim pieces of wood (or more, depending upon the height of your panel) as braces in the same manner. Braces are used to keep the

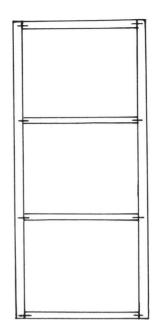

frame stable. Check to make sure all corners are square.

**3.** Measure, mark, and cut out a section of plywood the width and length of panel frame. Glue and nail plywood to one side of frame. Sand all rough edges.

## TO COVER SCREEN PANELS:

**1.**

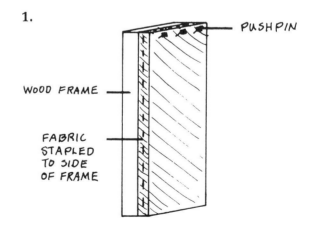

Working with one panel at a time, measure, mark, and cut out a section of fabric the length and width of panel plus 1″ extra all around. Place right side up, over open side of frame. Align pattern, use pushpin to hold fabric in place, then staple into position around sides of frame. Square fabric at each corner.

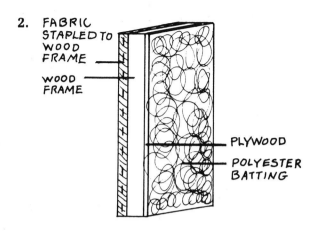

**2.** FABRIC STAPLED TO WOOD FRAME

WOOD FRAME

PLYWOOD

POLYESTER BATTING

Flip screen panel to uncovered side, plywood face up. Measure, mark, and cut out (use scissors, batting will dull fabric shears) a section of batting the exact length and width of one panel and lay it on top of plywood.

**3.**

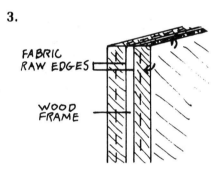

FABRIC RAW EDGES

WOOD FRAME

Measure, mark, and cut out a section of fabric the length and width of panel plus 1½″ extra all around. Carefully position fabric right side up over batting, and use pushpin to hold in place. Wrap fabric around to sides of frame (be careful not to pull it too taut—you don't want to lose the puffiness of the batting), and staple into position around the sides, squaring fabric at each corner. Trim away excess if fabric overlaps; raw edges should not touch.

**4.**

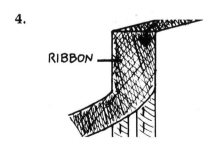

RIBBON

Using undiluted white household glue, attach ribbon to each side of each panel, covering staple heads and all raw edges of fabric.

**5.** When all screen panels are covered and trimmed, join them together with bifold hinges.

# GAME TABLETOP— BACKGAMMON

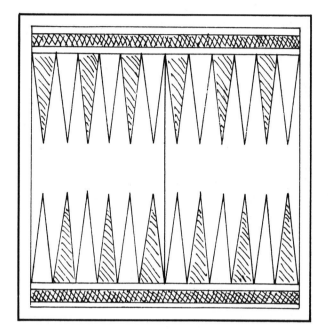

Backgammon is *the* popular game of the 1970s and 1980s. It is played with pieces on a double board in which the throwing of the dice determines the moves.

This game tabletop is 16″ square and is designed to fit on top of a 16″ square Parsons table. It is a slick decorator addition to any area.

### YOU NEED . . .

For a 16″ × 16″ backgammon board top:
**Fabric**—½ yard medium weight, 36″ wide for contrast color base
**Fabric**—½ yard medium weight, 36″ wide for game background
**Fabric**—½ yard medium weight, 36″ wide for light triangles
**Fabric**—¼ yard medium weight, 36″ wide for dark triangles
**Fabric**—¼ yard medium weight, 36″ wide for decorative print trim

**Construction paper**—3 sheets white, each 18″ × 24″
**Brown wrapping paper**—to catch excess glue
**Tape measure**
**Marking pencil**
**Fabric shears**
**Scissors**
**Spray adhesive**
**Iron**

If you want to make a game table, follow the basic Covered Parsons Table directions on page 20, then proceed with the game top using the following directions. If you want only a game board, work on a covered 16″ square of ¼″ thick plywood.

## TO MAKE IT . . .

**1.** Press all fabric flat. Trim off selvages. Work on a large smooth surface covered with brown wrapping paper (to catch excess glue). For contrast color base, measure, mark, and cut out a 15″ square of contrast color fabric. Center it and attach to tabletop or covered board with spray adhesive.

**2.**

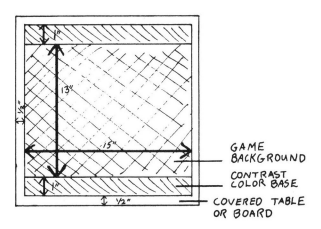

Measure, mark, and cut out a 16″ × 14″ rectangle of construction paper and game background fabric. Attach wrong side of fabric square to right side of paper square with spray adhesive. Allow to dry thoroughly. Trim rectangle down to 15″ × 13″. Center it, fabric side up, over contrast color base and attach with spray adhesive.

**3.**

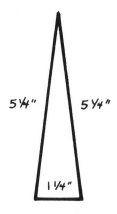

Attach light and dark fabrics to separate pieces of construction paper, each 9″ × 24″ with spray adhesive. Allow to dry thoroughly. Measure, mark, and cut out 12 light and 12 dark triangles, each 5¼″ × 5¼″ × 1¼″.

**4.**

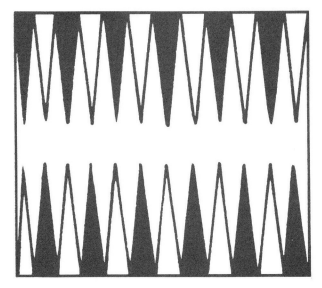

Glue light and dark triangles to background fabric in alternating order as illustrated.

**5.**

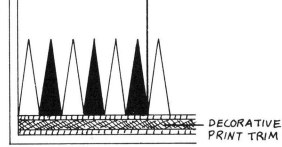

Finally, measure, mark, and cut out two strips of decorative print trim fabric, each 16″ × 1″.

Glue strips to paper and allow to dry thoroughly. Trim strips down to 15" × ½". Center strips on contrast colored base fabric and glue into position. Draw a line across center of board to divide it for playing.

To protect game board as a tabletop, cover it with a square of glass cut to size.

# GAME TABLETOP— CHECKERS

This game tabletop is 16" square and is designed to fit on top of a 16" square Parsons table. When you are not playing a game, the table is always ready to be used as a side table in any room.

## YOU NEED . . .

For a 16" × 16" checkerboard top:
**Fabric**—½ yard medium weight, 36" wide for contrast color base
**Fabric**—½ yard medium weight, 36" wide for light squares
**Fabric**—¼ yard medium weight, 36" wide for dark squares
**Fabric**—¼ yard medium weight, 36" wide for decorative print trim
**Construction paper**—1 sheet white, 18" × 24"
**Brown wrapping paper**—to catch excess glue
**Tape measure**
**Marking pencil**
**Fabric shears**

**Scissors**
**Spray adhesive**
**Iron**

If you want to cover a small table as a base for your checkerboard top, follow the basic directions for a Covered Parsons Table on page 20, then proceed with the game top using the following directions. If you want only a game board, work on a covered 16" square of ¼" thick plywood.

## TO MAKE IT . . .

**1.** Press all fabric flat. Trim off selvages. Work on a large smooth surface covered with brown wrapping paper. For game's base measure, mark and cut out a 15" square of contrast color fabric. Center it and attach to tabletop, or covered board, with spray adhesive.

**2.**

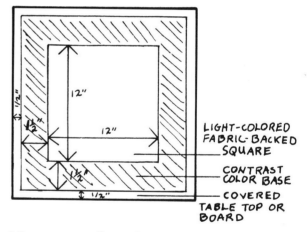

LIGHT-COLORED FABRIC-BACKED SQUARE
CONTRAST COLOR BASE
COVERED TABLE TOP OR BOARD

Measure, mark, and cut out a 13" square of both paper and light-colored fabric. Attach wrong side of fabric square to right side of paper with spray adhesive. Allow to dry thoroughly. Trim fabric-backed paper down to a 12" square. Center it, fabric side up, over contrast color base square and attach with spray adhesive. Measure, mark, and cut out a 9" square of both construction paper and dark-colored fabric. Attach wrong side of fabric square to right side of paper with spray adhesive. Allow to dry thoroughly.

**3.**

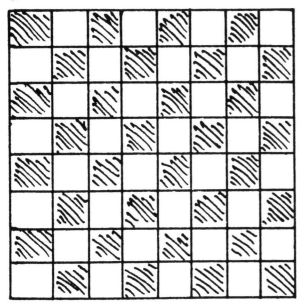

Measure, mark, and cut out 32 1½″ paper-backed dark-colored fabric squares. Using spray adhesive, attach to light-colored fabric as illustrated to create an alternating light and dark pattern.

**4.**

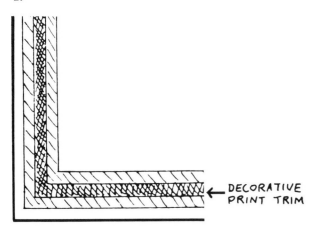

← DECORATIVE PRINT TRIM

Finally, measure, mark, and cut out a section of decorative print trim fabric 16″ × 5″. Glue strip to paper and allow to dry thoroughly. Cut fabric-backed section into four strips, each 14″ × ¾″. Center strips around and on top of contrast colored base fabric and glue into position, making sure you cut each end of each strip so that the raw edges butt together and form a mitered corner.

To protect game board as a tabletop, cover it with a square of glass cut to size.

# SHIRRED FOLDING SCREEN

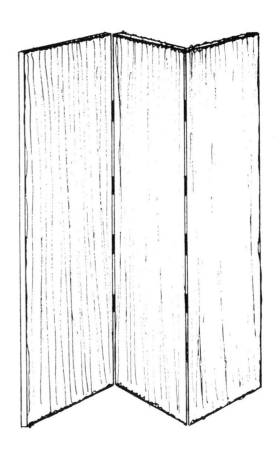

A wall covered with shirred screens, floor-to-ceiling or shorter, creates opulence and privacy when you want it, and adds a feeling of warmth during cool months. During warm months, or when you don't want that effect, simply fold it away out of sight.

To make a shirred screen, the basic principles of a shirred wall are put into practice.

### YOU NEED . . .

**1″ × 2″ pine frames**—no smaller than 12″ wide and as tall as you wish (If you are not into "building," your local lumberyard can easily make screen panels to your specifications.)
**Metal wood joiners**
**Hammer**
**Saw**

**Square**
**Wood glue**
**Brads** (headless nails)—¾″ inch long
**Sandpaper**—medium grid
**Fabric**—length and width of each panel + 1″ extra all around for flat side length; length of panel + 4″ and 2½ times the width for each shirred panel
**Tape measure**
**Marking pencil**
**Fabric shears**
**Scissors**
**Fusible bonding web**
**Package string**
**Pushpins**
**Staple gun and staples**
**Iron**
**Bifold hinges**—quantity depends upon height of screen. Ask your lumberyard.

## TO MAKE IT . . .

Have your local lumberyard construct screen panels for you, or make them yourself as follows:

**1.** To make one panel, measure, mark, and cut two pieces of 1″ × 2″ pine the height you desire and four pieces the width you desire.

**2.**

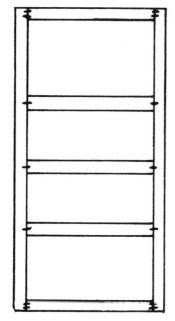

Make a panel by joining the two long side pieces of wood to the two short pieces as

illustrated. Make sure the 1″ side of wood faces up. Use metal wood joiners and glue to hold pieces together, and attach four interim pieces of wood (or more, depending upon the height of your panel) as braces in the same manner. Braces are used to keep the frame stable. Check to make sure all corners are square.

## TO COVER SCREEN PANELS:

**1.**

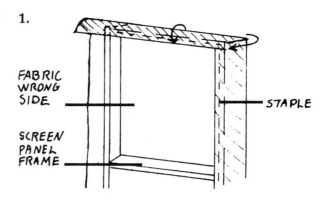

FABRIC WRONG SIDE

SCREEN PANEL FRAME

STAPLE

Working with one panel at a time, measure, mark, and cut out a section of fabric the length and width of panel plus 1″ extra all around. Place fabric over one side of frame, right side up. Align pattern, use pushpin to hold fabric in place, then staple into position around to opposite side of frame. Square fabric at each corner.

**2.** Flip screen panel to uncovered side and set aside.
For each panel measure, mark, and cut out a section of fabric 4″ longer than the panel and 2½ times the width of the panel.

**3.**

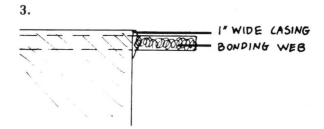

1″ WIDE CASING
BONDING WEB

Press all raw side edges under ½″.
Fold top raw edge under 2″ and press in place. Measure, mark, and cut strips of fusible bonding web 1″ long and as wide as the fabric

you are working with (use scissors, the bonding web will dull your fabric shears). Fuse fabric along bottom raw edge of turn under as illustrated, following manufacturer's directions. You now have a top casing 1″ wide.

**4.**

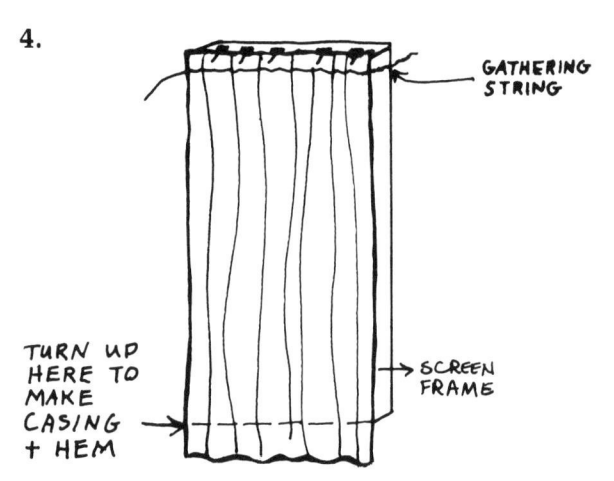

GATHERING STRING

TURN UP HERE TO MAKE CASING + HEM

SCREEN FRAME

Carefully thread package string through casing and use pushpins to hold gathered fabric in place along top of screen panel. Measure and mark where casing should be along bottom of panel.

**5.** Remove shirred fabric from screen panel. Turn bottom raw edge under as marked and use fusible bonding strips to create a casing as previously directed.

**6.** Thread bottom casing with package string. Use pushpins to hold shirred fabric in place on screen panel. Align pattern, then staple in place along top and bottom edges. Make sure staples go into the wood vertically.

**7.** When all screen panels are covered, join them together with bifold hinges.

# WRAP AND TIE ROOM

*This is a super-fast and lighthearted way to decorate. Simply wrap all of your furniture in sheets or fabrics and tie with grosgrain ribbons. Perfect for a summer house, or when you're between slipcovers, or just for fun.*

## NO-SEW PROJECTS

*Window Swags*
*Wrap and Tie Chair Cover*
*Wrap and Tie Ottoman Cover*
*Wrap and Tie Flower Box*
*Wrap and Tie Pillow*

## WINDOW SWAGS

A refreshing change from draperies or curtains is to swag a window. Attach drapery tiebacks just above or at top of window frame following manufacturer's directions. Measure the length and width of the window you wish to enhance and cut your fabric accordingly. Carefully drape fabric over window frame so that it rests on the tiebacks. Arrange it into pleasing folds and cut sides to effect a jabot.

If you have to join two pieces of fabric together to create one long piece, join them with safety pins and hide the center seam by placing a colorful shawl or contrasting fringed piece of fabric over the tiebacks as shown. (If you wish a monotone effect, use the same color fabric.)

If you have a brass or wooden drapery rod across the top of your window and don't want heavy draperies interrupting cool breezes during the hot summer months, but want a touch of "something," do the following:

Measure, mark, and cut out a rectangle of fabric, two to three times the width of your window. Leave the raw edges alone or attach decorative fringe, braid, or ribbon to them with the aid of fusible bonding web.

Nail one end of rectangle to wall directly

behind drapery rod finial. Drape fabric around rod, loosely stretching it out across the width of your window as illustrated. Nail other end of fabric to wall directly behind second drapery rod finial.

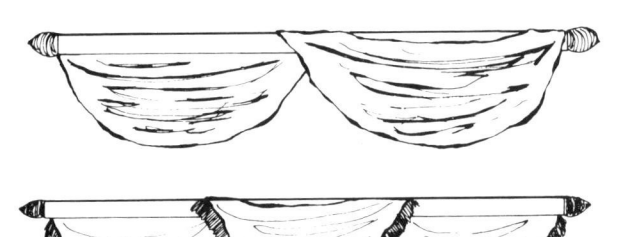

## WRAP AND TIE CHAIR COVER

Two king-size flat sheets, fabric shears, pinking shears, and ribbons in three assorted colors are all you need to cover a small club chair.

Press sheets flat, then place them together and work with them as one (this gives added richness to your finished cover).

Center sheets over club chair and tuck deeply in and around cushion. Smooth sheets along arms so that center back of chair is filled with gathers. Gather in excess sheeting at each corner and at center back of chair. Cut slits at each side of gathers. Thread ribbons through slits and tie them into bows. Trim excess sheeting from around base of chair with pinking shears.

## WRAP AND TIE OTTOMAN COVER

Because this ottoman is square, you will need two squares of fabric to cover it. Figure the size of the fabric needed by measuring ottoman up from the floor, across the center top, and down to the floor. This will give you the measure for one side of the fabric square.

Press fabric flat, then place squares together and work with them as one (this gives added richness to your finished cover), right side up. Center fabric over ottoman. Wrap ribbon or colored cords around ottoman as shown. Smooth top and gather excess fabric to corners. Trim excess fabric from around base of ottoman with pinking shears.

# WRAP AND TIE FLOWER BOX

When you are working with flowers and don't seem to have "just the right container" for them, you can always improvise by covering a cardboard box with two pieces of fabric in a color which compliments your flowers *and* your room setting.

Measure, mark, and cut out two squares of fabric. Each square should be approximately three times the size of the largest side of the box you are going to cover. Tie the two squares of fabric together at opposite corner points as illustrated.

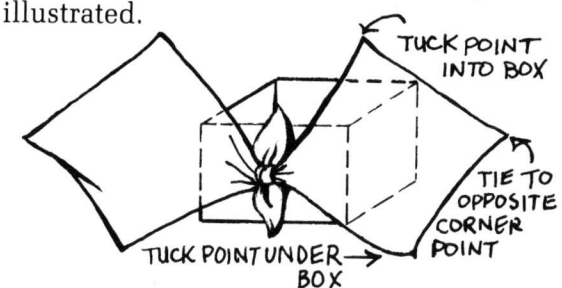

Wrap tied squares around box. Tie opposite corners together and tuck top and bottom corners into and under the box.

Fill an ordinary glass jar with your favorite flowers and place in the box.

# WRAP AND TIE PILLOW

This is really instant accessorizing. Depending upon the fabric used, velvet, satin, glazed cotton, burlap, and so on, the effect can be one of formal elegance or country casual.

## YOU NEED . . .

**Pillow**—square or round, any size
**Fabric**—light, medium- or heavyweight, 3 to 4 times the size of pillow to be covered
**Tape measure**
**Marking pencil**
**Fabric shears**
**Pinking shears**
**Iron**

## TO MAKE IT . . .

**1.** Press fabric flat. Trim off selvages.

**2.**

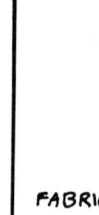

Measure, mark, and cut out a section of fabric 3 to 4 times the size of pillow you wish to cover. Place square pillow diagonally on top of wrong side of fabric square, as illustrated.

**3.**

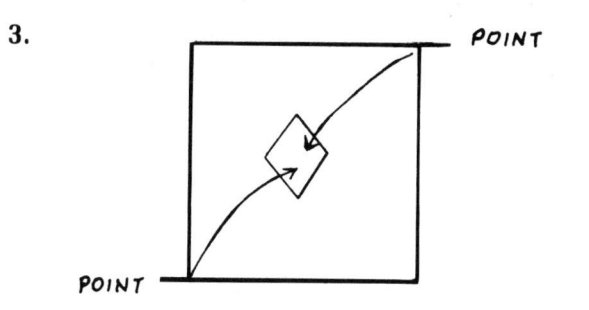

Tie opposite points of fabric together. Fan out ties and tuck raw edges under.

**4.**

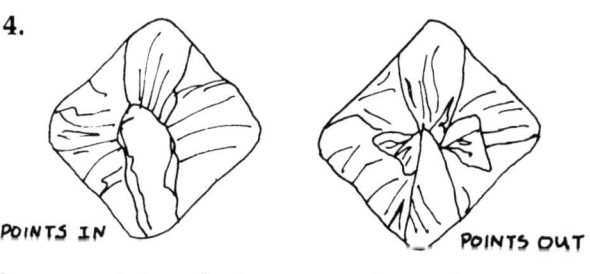

Leave point ends in or out depending upon the effect you want to achieve.

# LIVING ROOM

A living or sitting room in the country or the city takes on a special glow when the entire space is decorated in one beautiful design. It's different . . . makes decorating easy and the room feel very special.

## NO-SEW PROJECTS

*Covered Lambrequin*
*Fabric Area Rug*
*Light Box Picture*
*Fabric-Covered Walls—Stapled*

## COVERED LAMBREQUIN

This is a bed or window treatment that is actually a cornice with sides which are shaped or straight and usually fabric covered.

Sometimes the sides are imitated in carvings to resemble draperies.

Here, as a window treatment, it is used to make a window area appear smaller or larger and to conceal drapery hardware. A lambrequin makes a dramatic decorating statement in any room, and when padded and covered it is an aid in diminishing outside noises.

### YOU NEED . . .

**Plywood**—½" thick, cut to size and shape you desire at lumberyard

**Fabric**—medium- to heavyweight. Amount needed depends upon size of lambrequin to be covered. You need enough to cover face and sides of lambrequin in one or three pieces of fabric with a 2" turn under.

**Polyester batting**—enough to cover face and sides of lambrequin with a 1" turn under

**Tape measure**

**Marking pencil**

**Fabric shears**

**Pushpins**

**Staple gun and staples**
**Iron**
**Hammer**
**Screwdriver**
**Wood glue**
**Common nails**—1½″ long (four penny) resin coated
**Screws**
**Angle irons**

## TO MAKE IT . . .

**1.** Take measurement and/or a drawing of what you want to your local lumberyard. Have them cut plywood to your requirements. When figuring how much wood you need, remember that the top of the lambrequin can or cannot go to the ceiling—that is up to you. Sides should be deep enough to accommodate drapery hardware plus ease space for removal of draperies or curtains (approximately 6″ to 8″).

**2.** Using wood glue and common nails, assemble lambrequin. Place it at window to make sure the size is correct and that it gives the architectural effect you desire before proceeding further.

**3.**

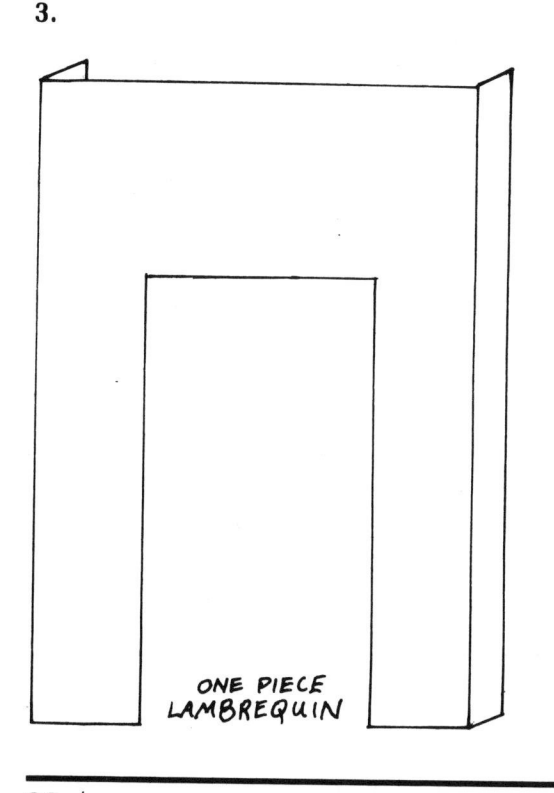

ONE PIECE LAMBREQUIN

THREE SECTION LAMBREQUIN (CONSTRUCTED WHEN WINDOW AREA IS EXCEPTIONALLY LARGE OR WHEN FABRIC IS NOT WIDE ENOUGH)

Wrap polyester batting around face and sides of wooden frame (or sections) and staple in place on wrong side.

**4.** Press fabric flat. Trim off selvages.

**5.**

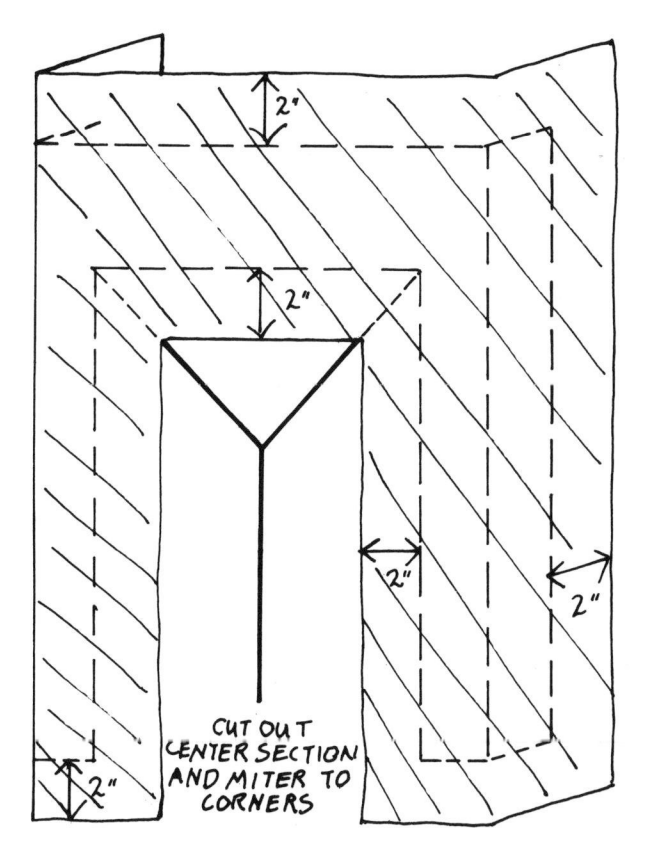

2″
2″
2″
2″
2″

CUT OUT CENTER SECTION AND MITER TO CORNERS

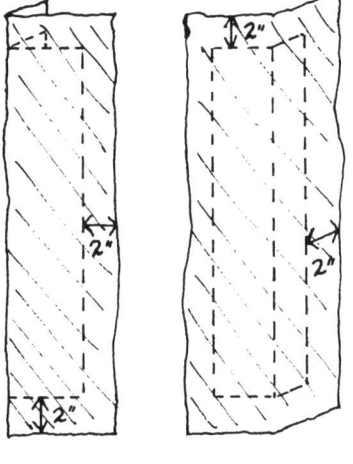

THREE SECTION LAMBREQUIN

Measure, mark, and cut out a section (or sections) of fabric the length and width of padded frame plus 2″ extra all around. Center fabric, right side up, over face of frame and secure with pushpins to hold in place. Cut out center section of fabric allowing a 2″ excess around inner perimeter of frame. Miter to inner corners.

If you are working with three separate sections of the frame, cover each individually, being careful to match fabric repeat accurately where sections will be joined.

**6.**

MITERED CORNER

Pull fabric taut over batting and staple in place on wrong side of wooden frame (or frame sections). Miter all corners and make sure fabric is smooth on face of frame.

**7.** Assemble three section frame following lumberyard's directions to create one solid piece.

Attach covered lambrequin to window area with screws and angle irons.

# FABRIC AREA RUG

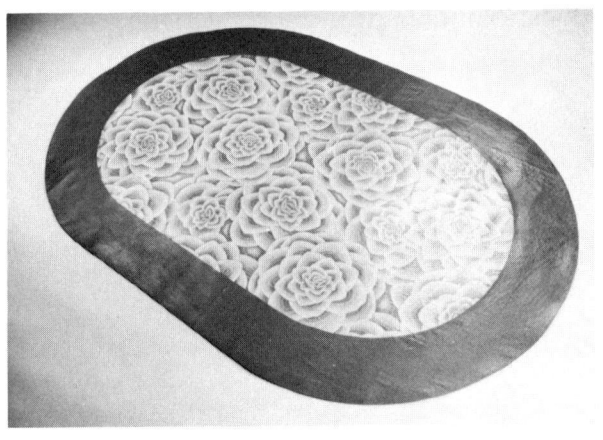

This rug can be made in any size up to 6′ × 6′ (primed artist's canvas is 6′ wide and sold by the yard in art supply stores).

The following directions are for an oval area rug 46″ × 72″.

### YOU NEED . . .

**Artist's canvas**—1⅓ yards, primed
**Fabric**—2½ yards medium weight solid color, 54″ wide
**Fabric**—2 yards medium weight, 44″ wide with all-over print motif
**Brown wrapping paper**—to make patterns
**Tape measure**
**Marking pencil**
**Scissors**
**Fabric shears**
**Acrylic sealer**
**Vinyl-to-wall adhesive**
**Pushpins**
**Plastic drop cloths**—to protect floor

**Paintbrush**—3″ wide
**Iron**

### TO MAKE IT . . .

**1.** Press all fabric flat. Trim off selvages.

**2.** Measure, mark, and cut out a canvas oval, 46″ × 72.″

**3.** Measure, mark, and cut out (use scissors, paper will dull your fabric shears) a brown paper oval 6½″ smaller than large canvas oval. Using paper oval as your pattern, cut out an oval from your print fabric the same size as your paper pattern.

**4.**

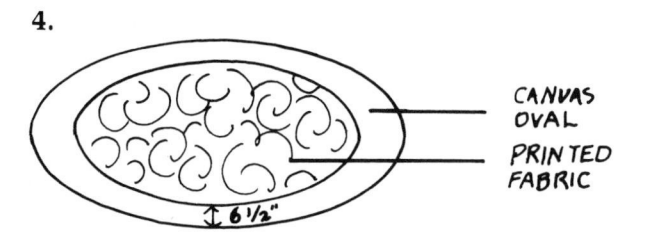

Cover floor with drop cloths and work on top of them.
With right sides up, paste printed fabric oval in exact center of canvas oval using vinyl-to-wall adhesive. Brush acrylic sealer onto face of both, making sure center oval does not shift its position as you do so.

**5.**

Measure, mark, and cut out a brown paper pattern for the border of rug which is large enough to allow for a ½″ overlap on inner edge and a 2″ overlap on outer edge of rug. Place paper pattern on top of solid color fabric and cut out rug border.
With right sides up, place fabric border on top of canvas rug allowing a ½″ overlap onto printed fabric and a 2″ overlap beyond outer edge of canvas. Turn and paste raw edges under and notch where necessary. Paste in place with vinyl-to-wall adhesive. Brush acrylic sealer over entire face of rug. Allow to dry thoroughly—overnight if possible.

# LIGHT BOX PICTURE

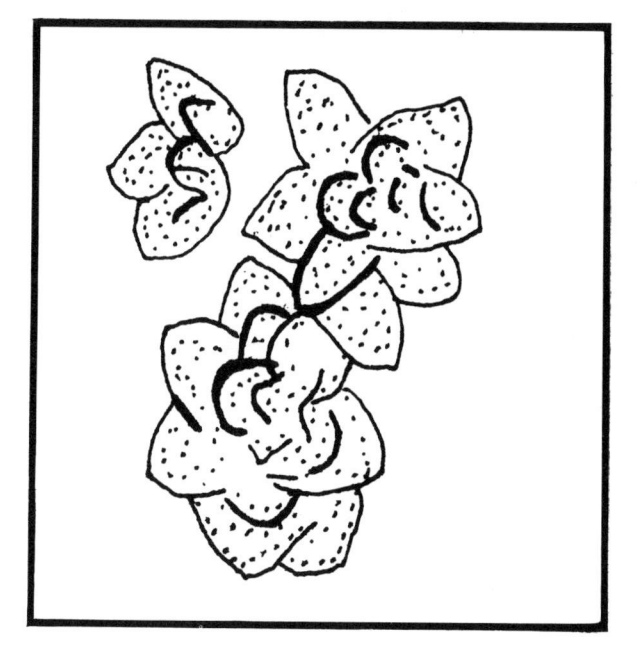

This is a pretty idea for a living room, dining room, child's room, or any area where you wish to add a bit of soft lighting.

### YOU NEED . . .

**4 artist's wooden stretcher bars**—to create any size rectangle or square frame
**Fabric**—medium-weight, enough to stretch over frame you create
**Fabric motifs**—for cutting out fruit, flowers, birds, animals, objects, and so on
**Tape measure**
**Marking pencil**
**Fabric shears**
**Pushpins**
**Staple gun and staples**
**Plastic drop cloth**
**Acrylic sealer**
**Sponge paintbrush**

Waxed paper
Single-edge razor blade
Miniature Christmas tree lights
Iron

## TO MAKE IT . . .

**1.**

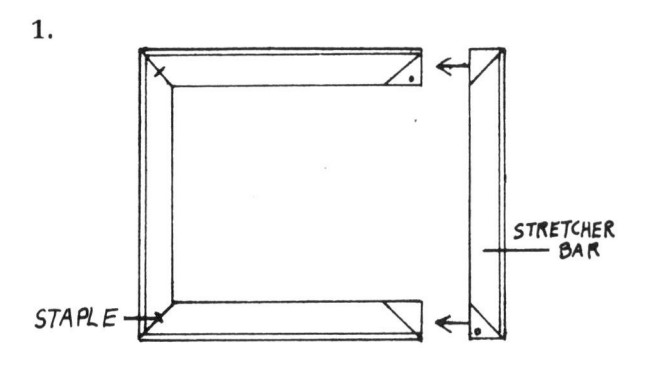

Following manufacturer's directions, push stretcher bars together to form a frame. Staple each corner as illustrated to keep frame stable.

**2.** Press fabric flat. Trim off selvages.
Measure, mark, and cut out a section of solid color fabric 4″ wider and 4″ longer than the assembled frame.

**3.** Center solid color fabric, right side up, on top of right side of frame. Hold fabric in place with pushpins.

**4.**

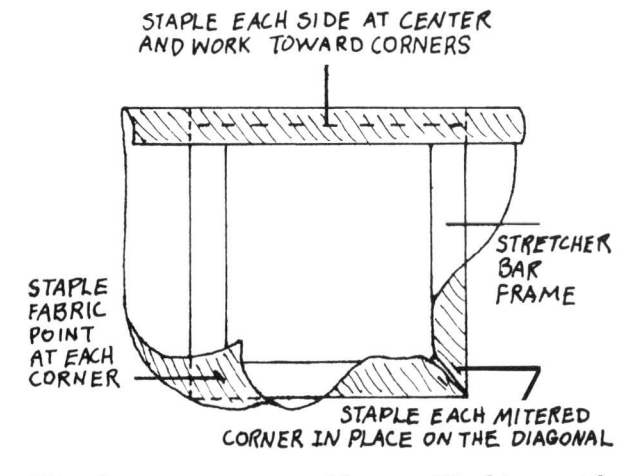

Flip frame to wrong side up. Working with one side at a time, pull fabric taut and staple in center of each side. Then staple toward corners. To do each corner, pull fabric down

toward center of frame from corner point and staple in place. Fold corners in and staple in place on the diagonal forming a miter. Trim away any excess fabric extending beyond the frame's inner edges.
Working on top of plastic drop cloth, brush one coat of acrylic sealer over entire surface of stretched fabric. Allow to dry thoroughly.

**5.** Carefully cut out fabric motif or motifs. Place them on waxed paper, then brush them with one coat of acrylic sealer. Allow to dry thoroughly.

**6.** Position cut-outs on top of stretched fabric. Apply one coat of acrylic sealer to the face of your picture to hold the cut-outs in place. Allow to dry for 30 minutes. Now apply ten more coats of acrylic sealer in alternating horizontal and vertical directions each time you do so. Allow a 30 minute drying period between each application.

**7.**

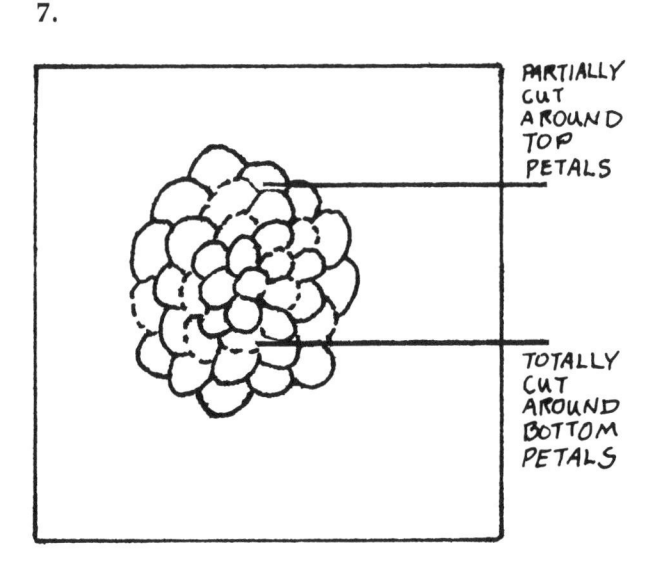

When picture is thoroughly dry (overnight is best), with a razor blade slit around area of the motif you wish to stand out from the solid color background. Follow illustration and be careful not to slit around outside edges of motif and not to slit through the solid color fabric. Pinch freed areas to make them curl and stand away from the background. They will curl more automatically with aging.
If your motif is something other than a flower (animal, boat, tree, etc.), calculate carefully

where you want light to come through before cutting.

8.

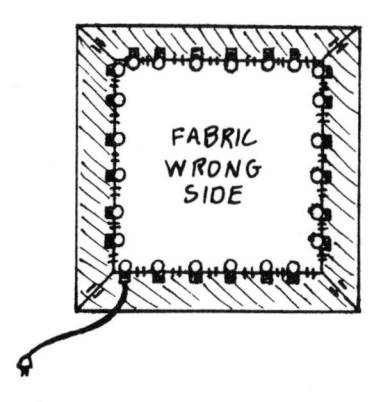

FABRIC WRONG SIDE

Flip picture to wrong side and staple miniature Christmas tree lights around back of frame. Hang picture, then plug it in and enjoy!

# FABRIC-COVERED WALLS—STAPLED

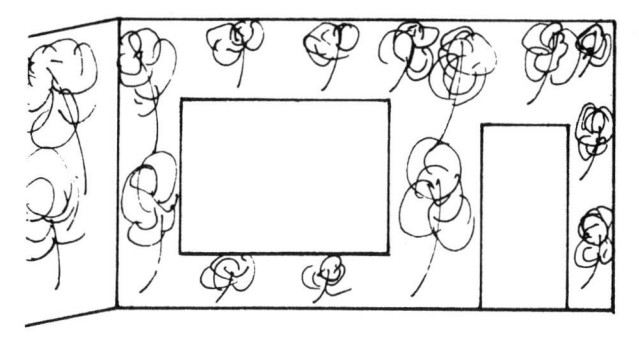

This method is easy to do and the fabric is easy to remove. Staples come out quickly with the aid of a screwdriver. Just remember to protect your eyes during removal. Fabric, if washable, can be hand- or machine-washed and reused for other projects.

## YOU NEED . . .

**Walls**—white or off-white; can have small bumps, cracks, or be textured
**Fabric**—small or large all-over design, random print or stripe, medium-weight
**Wood lattice stripping**—1″ wide by ¼″ thick, enough to go around perimeter of area to be covered. Don't forget to go around doors, windows, and down both sides of corners (stripping is used as a protection for your walls and can or cannot be used, the choice is yours).

**Saw**
**Finishing nails** (headless nails)
**Hammer**
**Chalk**
**String**—as long as wall is high + 12″
**Heavy weight**—to tie to end of string
**Tape measure**
**Marking pencil**
**Fabric shears**
**Pushpins**
**Staple gun and staples**
**Upholsterer's tacking tape**
**Iron**

## TO MAKE IT . . .

1.

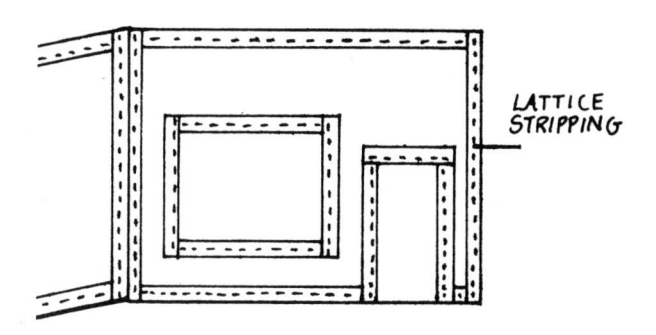

LATTICE STRIPPING

Measure, mark, and cut lattice stripping to proper size, then nail it around perimeter of area to be covered as illustrated.

2. To figure how much fabric you need, measure height and width of area to be covered (do not subtract for door or window openings). Add 4″ extra all around to allow for pattern seaming and alignment. If fabric you are using has an obvious repeat, add one extra repeat in length to your requirements.
Press fabric flat. Trim off selvages. Measure, mark, and cut fabric into panels each as wide as needed and each equal to height of wall plus 4″.

**3.** To establish the true vertical line of your wall for positioning fabric correctly, plumb line it. Thumbtack a piece of chalked string to the spot where the ceiling meets the wall and where you will staple your first length of fabric. Tie a heavy weight (rock, washer, hammer, etc.) to the end of the string near the floor to keep it taut. Hold the weight in place with one hand or foot and snap the chalked string with your other hand. If you have kept everything steady, the chalked line on the wall is the true vertical.

**4.** Allowing 2″ extra fabric at the top of wall area to be covered, begin in a corner and use pushpins to hold fabric to lattice stripping at 6″ intervals. Align fabric design. Trim excess fabric down to ½″.

**5.** If you feel having the staples show is objectionable, color their heads to match fabric's background with shoe polish, nail polish, or Magic Marker before dropping them into the staple gun.

Double check to make sure fabric is perfectly aligned. Working out from center of wall toward corners, staple fabric into position across top of wall, turning raw edges under ½″ as you do so and placing staples approximately 1″ apart. As you work, gently pull and smooth out wrinkles—do not make the fabric too taut.

**6.**

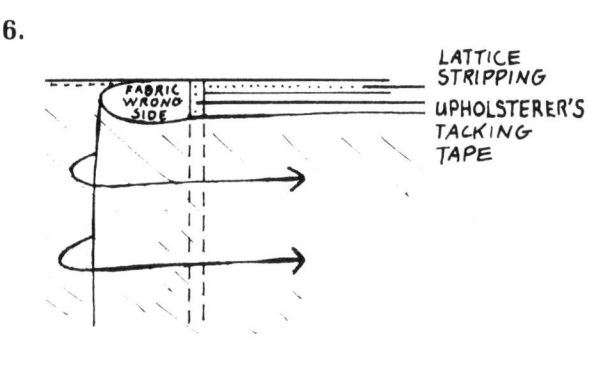

When fabric panels are to be joined together, lattice stripping must be nailed to the wall where seams will be. After lattice stripping is nailed in place down the length of the wall, join fabric panels together using upholsterer's tacking tape to make a back tacked seam. Staple first panel in place on top of lattice stripping along fabric's raw edge. Place second panel on top of first, right sides together, and matching repeats. Staple along raw edge to hold fabric in alignment. Place and staple upholsterer's tacking tape on top of stapled raw edges. Turn panel right side out and pull over tape. Repeat this procedure with the addition of each fabric panel.

When stapling fabric down the sides of the walls, try to staple down each simultaneously to keep fabric in alignment. If fabric does not begin and end in a corner, but goes around it, staple down both sides of the corner to keep fabric in alignment and to achieve the proper indentation.

**7.** The last area to be stapled is along the baseboard. If you have inadvertently stretched the fabric, creating an excess while stapling it in place, make tiny tucks all along the baseboard area as you turn raw edges under.

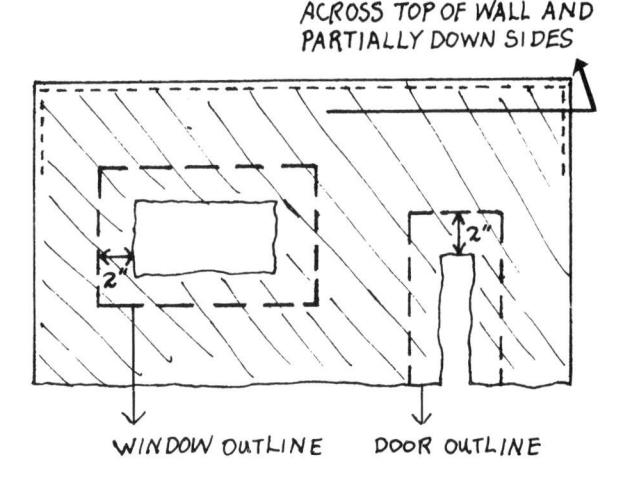

(If you end up with a "clump" of fabric in one area of the baseboard, place a piece of furniture or a plant in front of it—no one will ever notice!)

When you have windows and doors to contend with, follow basic wall stapling directions in steps 1 through 6. Note that when stapling in this manner you have totally covered any doors or windows with fabric. Now treat your wall area as a giant pumpkin, and using fabric shears, cut out the window and door areas leaving a 2″ fabric excess around the insides of their perimeters. Turn all raw edges under around window and door frames and staple in place.

For a more formal effect attach grosgrain ribbon or braid on top of staples using undiluted white household glue.

# BATHROOM

A bathroom with a personality . . . pillowcase curtains and a floor-to-ceiling shower curtain which can also double as a spare sheet when that extra guest arrives and your linen closet is bare.

## NO-SEW PROJECTS

*Cardboard Picture Frames*
*Covered Wooden Picture Frame*
*Floor-to-Ceiling Shower Curtain*
*Pillowcase Window Curtains*
*Standard Length Shower Curtain*
*Upholstered "What-Not" Box*

## CARDBOARD PICTURE FRAMES

Mini easel-backed frames, perfect for pictures or mirrors, make thoughtful gifts to give . . . or to keep.

### YOU NEED . . .

**Fabric**—12″ squares, medium-weight
**Cardboard** or #80 Bainbridge illustration board
**Polyester fleece padding**
**Steel ruler**
**Marking pencil**
Mat knife
Fabric shears
White household glue
Small disposable container
Paintbrush—1″ wide
Heavy books
Iron
Optional—soutache or similar trim

### TO MAKE IT . . .

**1.** Press fabric flat. Trim off selvages.

**2.** Measure, mark, and cut out cardboard (use a mat knife) in the shapes you desire, or use the sizes and shapes of the ones shown.

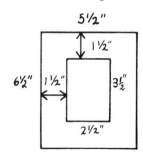

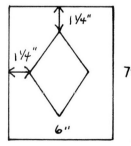

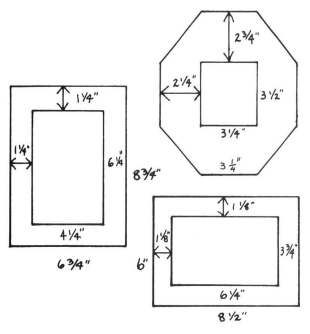

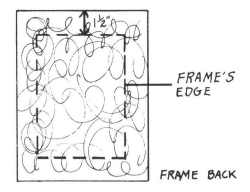

Measure, mark, and cut out two sections of fabric, each 1½″ larger all the way around than the size of your frame. Measure, mark, and cut

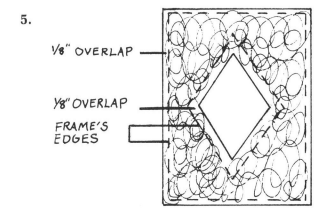

FRAME BACK

out the center of one fabric section as illustrated, allowing 1½″ to 1¾″ to extend beyond inside edges of center opening on face of frame.

**3.** Measure, mark, and cut out frame backs the same size as frame fronts, but without the center opening.

**4.** To make an easel leg for the back of your frame, measure, mark, and cut out a strip of cardboard 1″ wide and 1″ shorter than the height of the frame. Using a mat knife, cut halfway through the strip 1″ down from its top—this will enable the easel leg to move.

## TO MAKE ONE PICTURE FRAME:

**1.** Measure, mark, and cut out cardboard sections, then measure, mark, and cut out a section of polyester fleece padding ⅛″ larger than your cardboard frame.

**2.**

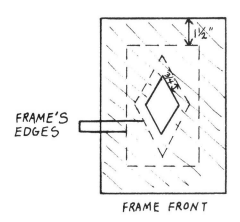

FRAME FRONT

**3.** Now measure, mark, and cut out two sections of fabric, each the same size as the front and back of your frame. Cut out the center of one fabric section to measure the same size as the center opening of cardboard frame's face. These are the linings. You will back each frame section to facilitate sliding picture in.

**4.** Measure, mark, and cut out a section of fabric 2½″ wide and 1″ longer than the cardboard easel leg.

**5.**

Pour white household glue into a small disposable container—do not dilute.
Brush glue over entire face of front section of cardboard frame and adhere polyester padding to it, overlapping outer edges. Cut out center, ⅛″ smaller than the opening.

**6.**

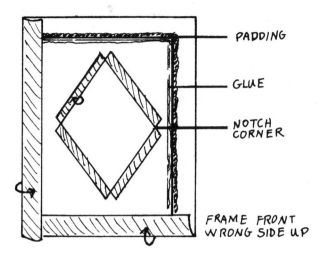

PADDING

GLUE

NOTCH CORNER

FRAME FRONT WRONG SIDE UP

Place front section of fabric, right side up, on top of padding, and holding all in place, flip to wrong side up. Brush glue around outer and inside edges of frame. Fold over raw edges of fabric and hold them in place with a heavy book while they dry.

**7.** Glue exact size section of fabric to wrong side of frame's face.

**8.**

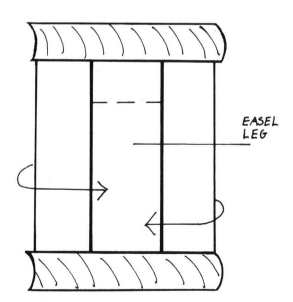

EASEL LEG

Now cover and glue remaining fabric sections to frame's back as previously instructed and cover easel leg as illustrated.

**9.** To join front and back sections of frame together, place both on a smooth flat surface, insides up. Brush glue around three sides of each frame section leaving a top or bottom untouched. Allow them to become a bit tacky,

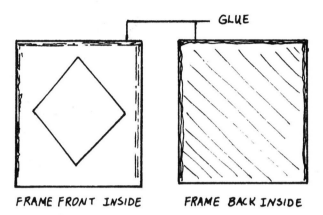

GLUE

FRAME FRONT INSIDE

FRAME BACK INSIDE

then carefully place one section on top of the other. Place a heavy book on top of frame to hold it in place while drying.

**10.** Glue soutache braid around perimeter of covered frame, being careful not to cover the frame's top or bottom opening. Allow to dry thoroughly. Finally glue covered easel leg to back of picture frame as follows: Apply glue to easel leg above scored point. Align the bottom of the leg with the center bottom of your picture frame and push glued area onto back of frame. Hold or weight it in place until thoroughly dry.

When thoroughly dry, your covered cardboard picture frame is ready to use as a mini-mirror or to hold your favorite photo.

# COVERED WOODEN PICTURE FRAME

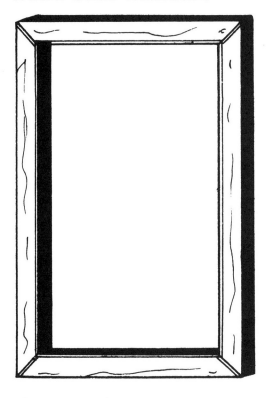

This is a quick, easy way to add a decorator look to an old mirror or picture frame.

## YOU NEED . . .

**Wooden frame**—for a mirror or a picture
**Fabric**—medium-weight, enough to cover front and back of each side of frame
**Spray paint**—flat white
**Tape measure**
**Marking pencil**
**Fabric shears**
**White household glue**
**Small disposable container**
**Paintbrush**—2″ wide
**Soutache or similar trim**

## TO MAKE IT . . .

**1.** Press fabric flat. Trim off selvages.

**2.** Remove mirror (or glass) and backing from frame.

**3.** Spray paint frame flat white. Allow to dry thoroughly before continuing with this project.

**4.**

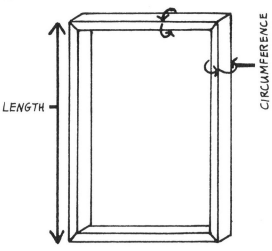

To figure how much fabric you need to cover each side of the frame, measure the circumference and length of each and add ½″ all around. Measure, mark, and cut out four sections of fabric accordingly.

**5.** Pour white household glue into disposable container and, if necessary, dilute with a tiny bit of water so that it spreads easily and evenly with a paintbrush.

**6.**

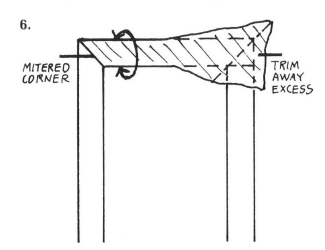

Working with one side at a time, brush glue onto frame, front and back. Wrap fabric around frame and trim away excess as illustrated to conform with the frame's mitered corner. Allow to dry thoroughly.

7.

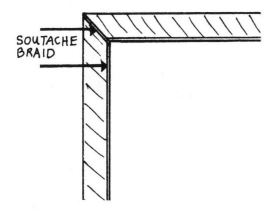

SOUTACHE BRAID

As a final finishing touch to your frame, embellish it with soutache or a narrow ribbon trim glued in place over seams and around inner edge of frame.

# FLOOR-TO-CEILING SHOWER CURTAIN

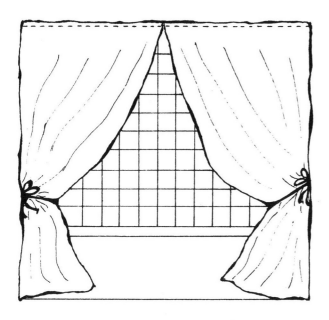

Making this shower curtain is so easy you may want to change it every week—well almost. Standard width shower curtains are 72″ wide. Therefore, your best bet here is to use a sheet—twin or full-size, depending upon how much fullness you desire.

**1 twin or full-size flat sheet**
**1 spring tension shower rod**
**Fusible bonding web**
**Tape measure**
**Marking pencil**
**Fabric shears**
**Pinking shears**
**Scissors**
**Iron**

## TO MAKE IT . . .

**1.** If sheet can be used upside down or if it has an attached border, the border can be used as the hem of your shower curtain as long as the design of the sheet is going in the right direction. Remember—flowers grow up from the ground, not down from the sky. Keep this in mind as you work and you won't make a mistake.

If the sheet you are working with doesn't have a definite design direction or an attached border, open top and bottom hems and press fabric flat. Do not trim off selvages.

**2.** Install spring tension shower rod at ceiling height over bathtub. If you have a stationary rod over your bath, leave it in place. You can use it to hang a shower curtain liner from. (If you have no shower curtain rod over your bath, you may want to use a second spring tension rod placed at a lower level to accommodate a liner.)

**3.**

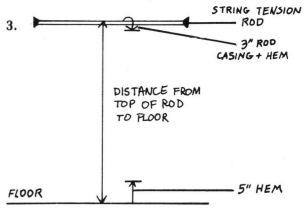

STRING TENSION ROD

3″ ROD CASING + HEM

DISTANCE FROM TOP OF ROD TO FLOOR

FLOOR

5″ HEM

To figure how long your fabric must be, measure distance from top of shower curtain rod to floor, add 5" (this is optional—your hem can be as narrow as 1" if you wish) for a bottom hem and 3" for a top casing and hem. Cut sheet down to correct size needed.

**4.**

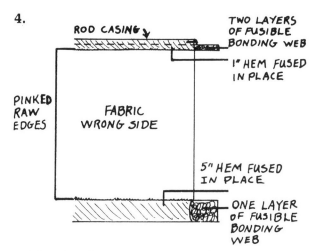

Fold what is to be the top of your shower curtain down 3" and press in place. Measure, mark, and cut out two strips of fusible bonding web (use scissors, bonding web will dull fabric shears) the width of the curtain and 1" long. Place fusible bonding web underneath pinked raw edge and fuse wrong side of raw edge to wrong side of curtain, following manufacturer's directions and as illustrated, to create a rod casing.

If border of sheet can be used as a hem, fine, you're all set. If it cannot, fold bottom of sheet up and trim off excess to create a 5" hem or less. Pink raw edge and press in place. Measure, mark, and cut a strip of fusible bonding web the depth of curtain's hem and the width of the curtain. Fuse hem in place following manufacturer's directions.

**5.** Remove spring tension shower rod from over bathtub. Remove rubber suction foot from one side of rod and very carefully slide shower curtain onto rod. Replace suction foot, reposition rod over bathtub, and twist it into place.

When a one-panel shower curtain is in use, care must be taken not to yank it and pull the fusing apart. If you have enough fabric, an alternative is to make two panels and create a dramatic curtained effect for your bath. Ribbon or cording tiebacks will allow movement without disturbing the rod casing across

the top. If you feel a liner is necessary, for a two-panel curtain, two should be used—one for each side. To hide the bit of stationary shower rod that may show, wrap and glue matching fabric, ribbon, or cording around it.

# PILLOWCASE WINDOW CURTAINS

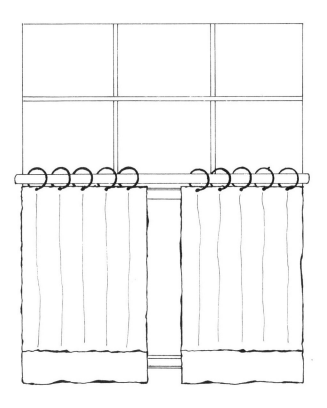

These curtains really are a magic trick. Simply attach clip-on café curtain hooks along the bottom (closed end) of two pillowcases. Thread onto café curtain rods and let them hang. You now have "instant" reversible window curtains. To create café curtains, use two sets of pillowcases, regular or king size—as many as you want, depending upon the height and width of your window.

This technique also works well with tea towels and hand towels.

# STANDARD LENGTH SHOWER CURTAIN

## YOU NEED . . .

**Fabric**—2½ yards light- to medium-weight, 72″ wide (or 1 twin or full-size flat sheet)
**Fusible bonding web**
**Tape measure**
**Marking pencil**
**Fabric shears**
**Pinking shears**
**Scissors**
**Iron**
**Large eyelets**—with attaching tool
**Shower curtain hooks**

## TO MAKE IT . . .

**1.** Press fabric flat. Trim off selvages and pink all raw edges.

**2.**

Measure, mark, and turn raw side edges of fabric under 1″. Press in place. Measure, mark, and cut out (use scissors, bonding web dulls fabric shears) two strips of fusible bonding web the length of the fabric and 1″ wide. Place bonding web underneath each pinked side edge and fuse wrong side of edges to wrong side of fabric, following manufacturer's directions.

Measure, mark, and turn top of fabric down 1½″. Press in place. Measure, mark, and cut out a strip of fusible bonding web 1½″ long and 70″ wide. Fuse hem in place as previously directed.

**3.**

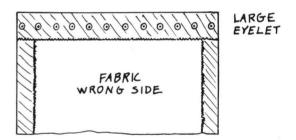

Using a shower curtain liner as your guide for proper spacing, mark top heading for large eyelets and attach them following directions on package.

**4.** Hang curtain. Measure and mark for length you desire, or follow the standard length of 72″. Remove curtain from shower hooks. Turn bottom raw edge under to create a 2″ wide hem. Trim away excess if necessary and press hem in place. Measure, mark, and cut out a strip of fusible bonding web the depth of curtain's hem and the width of the curtain. Fuse hem in place following manufacturer's directions.

**5.** Hang curtain for final time. Enjoy it! Remember, though, when using it, the curtain is only fused together, not stitched. It will withstand a certain amount of light tugging, but it is not as strong as if it had been sewn. Also, with continuous, heavy moisture the bonding may loosen. Cut a new strip as large as the opened section and re-fuse.

# UPHOLSTERED "WHAT-NOT" BOX

A pretty box for jewelry, special treasures, those "unmentionable" sewing supplies, or good old "what-nots."

## YOU NEED . . .

**Cardboard shoe box**—any size
**Fabric**—medium-weight, enough to cover the inside, outside, and top entirely plus 1″ extra all around
**Tape measure**
**Marking pencil**
**Steel ruler**
**Fabric shears**
**Dressmaker's pins**
**White household glue**
**Small disposable container**
**Paintbrush**—1″ wide
**Grosgrain ribbon**—1″ wide or wider and the length of the box
**Rattail cord**—enough to go around lid of box plus 1 yard extra
**Iron**

## TO MAKE IT . . .

**1.**

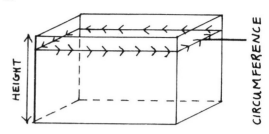

Measure, mark, and cut out two sections of fabric, each 1″ larger on all sides than the box's height and circumference.

**2.** Measure, mark, and cut out two sections of fabric, each ½″ larger on all sides than the box's bottom.

**3.** Measure, mark, and cut out five sections of fleece padding, each equal to one outer side and the outer bottom of box.

**4.** Pour white household glue into small disposable container.

**5.** Coat outside of box with glue. Adhere padding sections to their respective sides. Trim away any excess.

**6.**

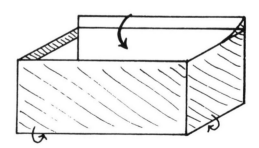

Starting at a back corner, wrap, pin to hold in place, then glue one fabric section around outside of box as illustrated. Tuck top edges in and bottom edges under and glue in place. Allow to dry thoroughly.

**7.** Measure, mark, and cut out two sections of fabric ½″ larger all around than the outside bottom of box. Turn raw edges of one section under to match bottom size of box and press. Glue section to box bottom. Hold it in place with pins and allow to dry thoroughly.

**8.**

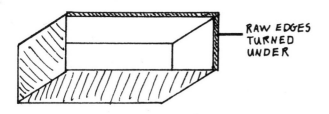

RAW EDGES
TURNED
UNDER

To line box use the second section of cut fabric. Turn raw edges of one long side under ½″ and press. Coat inside of box with glue and fit in lining. Make sure folded edge is at top of box. Turn raw edges under, press, and fit remaining bottom of box fabric section in place.

**9.**

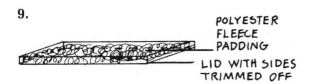

POLYESTER
FLEECE
PADDING

LID WITH SIDES
TRIMMED OFF

Cut off sides from box's top and trim lid to fit exactly on top of box. Measure, mark, and cut out a section of fleece padding the same size as the lid and glue in place on lid's top.

**10.** Measure, mark, and cut out two sections of fabric ¾″ larger all around than box lid. Glue one section, right side up, to top of box lid, wrapping and gluing raw edges to underside of lid as you do so.

**11.**

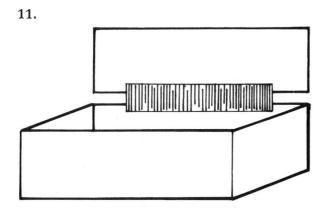

Measure, mark, and cut your grosgrain ribbon ½″ shorter than the length of box. Fold ribbon in half lengthwise and press. Glue ribbon in place—half on inside of box and half on inside of lid—as illustrated.

**12.** Turn raw edges of remaining fabric section under to fit underside of box lid. Press, then glue in place.

**13.**

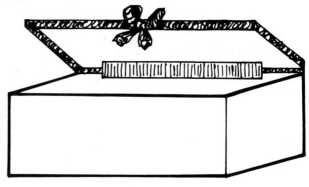

Beginning at center front of box lid, glue rattail cord around lid's edge. Leave ends long enough to tie a small bow.

*Right:* **Living room**

*Below:* **Framed towel**

*Bottom:* **Parsons game tables**

Right: **Bedroom**
Below: **Wrap-and-fan pillows**
Middle: **Gathered lampshade**
Bottom: **Dinette**
Opposite: **Wrap-and-tie room**

*Left:* **Dining room**
*Top:* **Director's chair cover**
*Above:* **Den**
*Opposite:* **Teen-age boy's room**

*Below:* **Child's room**
*Opposite top:* **Covered bolsters**
*Opposite bottom:* **Botanical place mats**

*Left:* **Bathroom**
*Top:* **Powder room**
*Middle:* **Fabric-covered boxes**
*Above:* **Fabric-covered picture frames**

# BEDROOM

A very romantic sitting/bedroom situation is easily created with shirred walls and round floor-length table skirts.

## NO-SEW PROJECTS

*Covered Cornice*
*Covered Pleated Lampshade*
*Gathered Dust Skirt*
*Tailored Dust Skirt*
*Oval Table Skirt*
*Round Floor-Length Table Skirt*
*Fabric-Covered Walls—Shirred*

## COVERED CORNICE

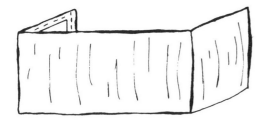

A cornice is a wooden border installed above a window as a finishing touch, or is used as a topping to conceal curtain or drapery rods.

### YOU NEED . . .

**Plywood**—½" thick
**Fabric**—light- to medium-weight, enough to cover the sides and front of cornice plus 2" extra all around
**Tape measure**
**Steel yardstick**
**Marking pencil**
**Saw**
**Nails**
**Hammer**
**Polyester fleece padding**
**Fabric shears**
**Staple gun and staples**

**Angle irons and screws—1"**
**Iron**

### TO MAKE IT . . .

**1.** Measure, mark, and saw plywood into three sections: a front and two sides. The front section should be cut so that its length equals 2" above top of curtain rod and 7" or less below bottom of curtain rod, and its width measures from curtain rod tip to curtain rod tip plus 4". The sides are each equal to the length of the front section with a depth from the wall plus 2½" to 3" out from front of curtain rod (6" to 7" in front if double rods are used).

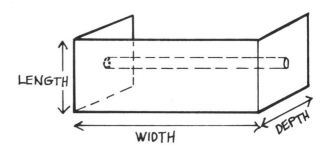

**2.**

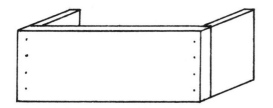

Nail sections together through front of cornice.

**3.**

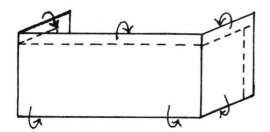

Measure, mark, and cut out a section of fleece padding large enough to wrap around entire cornice, as illustrated. Staple padding in place on wrong side of cornice. Clip padding and trim away excess where necessary.

**4.** Measure, mark, and cut out a section of fabric large enough to wrap around entire padded cornice. Follow same procedure for attaching fabric as you did for attaching padding.

**5.** Attach angle irons to top (and bottom edges if cornice is long) edges of cornice sides and follow manufacturer's directions for mounting cornice to wall.

# COVERED PLEATED LAMPSHADE

These directions apply to any size vinyl or paper pleated lampshade. Make sure the shade you are covering is smooth and white or off-white so that it will not change the color of the fabric you are working with.

### YOU NEED . . .

**Pleated lampshade**—vinyl or paper
**Fabric**—light- to medium-weight
**Tape measure**
**Marking pencil**
**Fabric shears**
**White household glue**
**Small disposable container**
**Paintbrush**—2″ wide
**Butter knife**
**Manicure scissors**
**Clear nail polish**
**Iron**

### TO MAKE IT . . .

**1.**

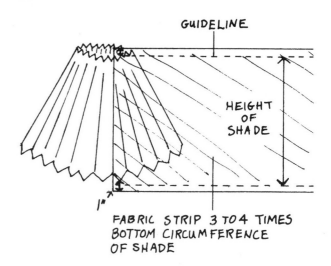

GUIDELINE

HEIGHT OF SHADE

1″

FABRIC STRIP 3 TO 4 TIMES BOTTOM CIRCUMFERENCE OF SHADE

To determine how much fabric you need, measure the height of the lampshade and its bottom edge circumference.
Press fabric flat. Trim off selvages.
Measure, mark, and cut out a strip of fabric 2″ longer than the height of shade and three to four times wider than the bottom circumfer-

ence measurement. It is not necessary to cut the fabric on the bias. It is also not necessary to have one long strip of fabric; you can use small sections just as easily. Lightly draw guidelines along top and bottom of fabric strip showing height of shade.

**2.** Pour white household glue into disposable container and, if necessary, dilute it with a tiny bit of water so that glue spreads easily and evenly with a paintbrush.

**3.** Beginning at seam of shade, brush glue into six pleats, being sure to get glue into all crevices deeply and evenly.

**4.**

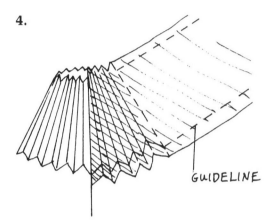

GUIDELINE

RAW EDGE OF FABRIC INSIDE
FIRST PLEAT AT SHADE'S SEAM

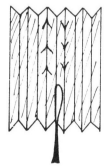

RUN BUTTER KNIFE BACK AND
FORTH IN PLEATS

Place raw edge of fabric strip inside first pleat. Follow guidelines for fabric alignment making sure that you always have 1″ extra fabric at the top and bottom of shade. Using the blunt edge of a butter knife and your fingers, press fabric as deeply as possible into the pleats. Run the knife in the pleats using back and forth

motions. (Always running the knife in the same direction tends to push the fabric out of the pleats and off the shade.) Wait about 10 minutes for the fabric to "set." (If glue comes through fabric, wipe off excess with a warm, damp sponge.) Continue gluing and attaching the fabric to the shade until it is completely covered. To be certain all fabric adheres smoothly, keep pressing the previously glued sections into the pleats with your fingers and the butter knife as you work around the shade. Your objective is to make the fabric "one" with the shade.

**5.**

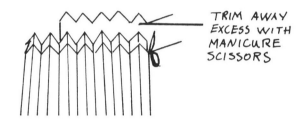

TRIM AWAY
EXCESS WITH
MANICURE
SCISSORS

When all pleats are covered, allow shade to dry thoroughly. Trim away excess fabric from top and bottom edges of shade with manicure scissors. Lightly brush all raw edges with clear nail polish to keep fabric from fraying.

# GATHERED DUST SKIRT

This is the easiest way I can think of to make a dust ruffle quickly in any size you need.

## YOU NEED . . .

**Fabric**—light- to medium-weight
**1 fitted sheet**—the size of the bed you are working with
**Tape measure**
**Marking pencil**
**Fabric shears**
**Scissors**
**Fusible bonding web**
**Package string**
**T-pins**
**Iron**

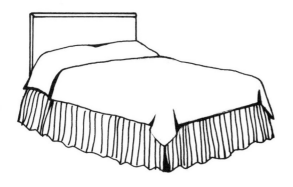

## TO MAKE IT . . .

**1.** Remove mattress from box spring and cover spring with a fitted sheet.

**2.** To figure how much fabric you need to make the dust skirt, measure the bed's side + end + side and multiply by 2½. This gives you the width of fabric needed. For length of fabric needed measure height from top of box spring to floor + 6".
Press fabric flat. Trim off selvages.
Measure, mark, and cut out fabric accordingly. If you must piece fabric to obtain the width you need, use strips of fusible bonding web and follow manufacturer's directions. (Use scissors to cut bonding web.)

**3.**

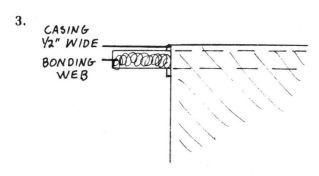

Working with one long piece of fabric, make a casing along top by turning raw edge under 1" and pressing crease in place.
Measure, mark, and cut strips of fusible bonding web ½" long and as wide as the fabric you are working with. Fuse fabric along bottom raw edge of turn under as illustrated and follow manufacturer's directions. You now have a top casing ½" wide.

**4.** Carefully thread package string through casing and T-pin (a large straight pin shaped like a "T") gathered fabric to top of covered box spring 2" in from outer edge. Measure and mark where hem should be along the bottom of dust skirt.

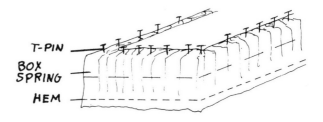

**5.** Remove skirt from box spring. Turn bottom raw edge under as marked and fuse in place with bonding web, following manufacturer's directions.

**6.** Carefully regather finished dust skirt. Arrange gathers and secure them in place on top of box spring 2" in from outer edge with T-pins.

**7.** Replace mattress on top of box spring.

---

# TAILORED DUST SKIRT

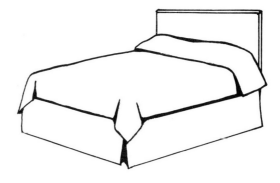

This uses much less fabric than the gathered dust ruffle and can also be made in less time.

## YOU NEED . . .

**Fabric**—light-, medium-, or heavyweight
**1 fitted sheet**—the size of the bed you are working with

Tape measure
Marking pencil
Fabric shears
Scissors
Pinking shears
Fusible bonding web
T-pins
Iron

## TO MAKE IT . . .

**1.** Remove mattress from box spring and cover spring with a fitted sheet.

**2.** To figure out how much fabric you need to make the dust skirt, measure the bed all the way around + 45″ for corner pleats and back seam overlap. This gives you the width of fabric needed. For the length, measure height from top of box spring to floor + 6″.
Press fabric flat. Trim off selvages.
Measure, mark, and cut out fabric accordingly. If you must piece fabric to obtain the width you need, use strips of fusible bonding web and follow manufacturer's directions. (Use scissors to cut bonding web.)

**3.** Pink top raw edge of fabric.

**4.** Measure and mark where hem should be along bottom of dust skirt.
Turn bottom raw edge under as marked. Trim excess fabric away to create the size hem you desire. Fuse hem in place with bonding web following manufacturer's directions.

**5.**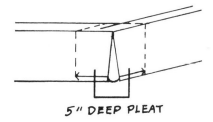

*5″ DEEP PLEAT*

Starting at the center of the head of bed, place pinked edge of tailored dust skirt on top of covered box spring 2″ in from outer edge. Hold in place with T-pins and make box pleated corners as illustrated.

**6.** Replace mattress on top of box spring.

# OVAL TABLE SKIRT

Oval table skirts usually look better short rather than to the floor. This is a personal opinion though and when the oval table to be covered is small, a floor-length cloth is quite acceptable. The eye does not absorb as much of the fabric with a small table and it will not overpower a decorating scheme the way a large floor-length oval table skirt might.

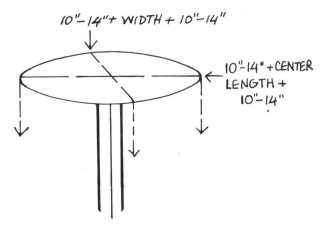

To figure the amount of fabric needed for a short cloth, measure center width and center length of your table plus 10″ to 14″ on each side for a drop.

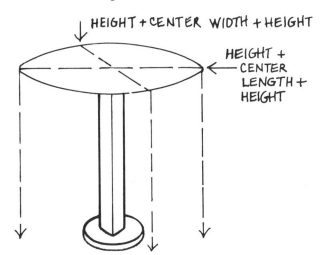

To figure the amount of fabric needed for a floor-length cloth, measure center width and center length plus two times the height of your table.

**TO MAKE IT . . .**

**1.** Press fabric flat. Trim off selvages.

**2.** Measure, mark, and cut out a rectangle of fabric in the length and width needed, plus 2″ extra all around.

**3.**

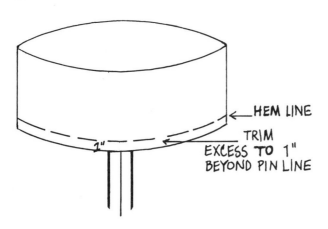

HEM LINE

TRIM EXCESS TO 1″ BEYOND PIN LINE

1″

Center fabric on top of table, right side up. Place heavy books on top of fabric to hold it steady and in position.
Measure and mark with pins where you wish hem to be on table skirt.
Trim excess fabric away around table skirt 1″ beyond pin line.
Remove heavy books.
Fold raw edges under and press fabric in place along pin line.
Remove pins, then hold hem in place with fusible bonding web, following manufacturer's directions.
(If you don't wish to hem your table skirt, use pinking shears and cut along pin line.)

# ROUND FLOOR-LENGTH TABLE SKIRT

This is easy to make and a quick way to dress up any area of a room in a hurry—especially if company is coming. These are basic directions for any size floor-length round table skirt. Remember, to make a round, you always begin

with a square (to make an oval, you always begin with a rectangle).

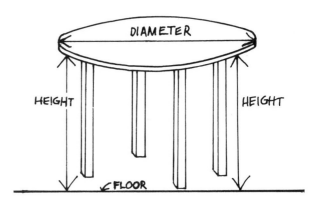

DIAMETER

HEIGHT          HEIGHT

FLOOR

To figure how much fabric you need, measure your table up from the floor, across the center top, and down to the floor again. This will give you the width of the fabric you need, and because you begin with a square this will also tell how long your fabric must be.

*YOU NEED . . .*

**Fabric**—light, medium-, or heavyweight, as wide as fabric measure indicates
**Tape measure**
**String**
**Marking pencil**
**Dressmaker's pins**
**Fabric shears**
**Pinking shears**
**Iron**

## TO MAKE IT . . .

**1.** Fold fabric square into quarters and place it on a large flat surface. Pin to hold fabric in alignment.

**2.** Transfer ½ of original measure (½ diameter + height) to a string compass (pencil tied to a string).

**3.**

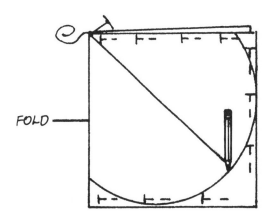

FOLD

Pin one end of string to fold point of fabric. Drop string down fold line. Hold pencil perfectly straight and carefully draw an arc.

**4.** Use pinking shears to carefully cut along line you have drawn. *Voila!* You now have a round floor-length table skirt!

If you wish to put a no-sew hem in your table skirt, add 2″ to your original measure when figuring how much fabric you need. After cutting out your circle, turn raw edges under 1″ or less and use fusible bonding web following manufacturer's directions to hold hem in place.

# FABRIC-COVERED WALLS—SHIRRED

This method requires a lot of fabric, but the result is well worth it. The effect is one of a rich coziness. This does make a room seem smaller, so be careful; if your room is very small, do only one wall this way and do the others flat.

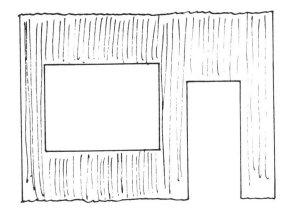

## YOU NEED . . .

**Walls**—any type will do
**Fabric**—small all-over design, random print, stripe or solid color, light- to medium-weight
**Wood lattice stripping**—1″ wide × ¼″ thick, enough to go around perimeter of area to be covered. Don't forget to go around doors and windows. (Stripping is used as a protection for your walls and can or cannot be used, the choice is yours.)
**Saw**
**Finishing nails** (headless nails)
**Hammer**
**Tape measure**
**Marking pencil**
**Fabric shears**
**Safety pins**
**Pushpins**
**Staple gun and staples**
**Iron**

## TO MAKE IT . . .

**1.**

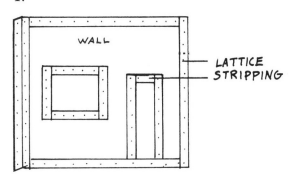

WALL

LATTICE STRIPPING

Measure, mark, and cut lattice stripping to proper size, then nail it around perimeter of area to be covered as illustrated. Lattice stripping is not needed in corners if you are shirring all four walls of the room.

**2.** To figure how much fabric you need, measure height of the wall plus 2″ extra at top and bottom (if fabric you are using has an obvious repeat, add one extra repeat in length to your requirements) and 2 to 3 times the width of area to be covered (height + 4″ and width × 2 or 3).

**3.** Press fabric flat. Do not trim off selvages. Measure, mark, and cut fabric into panels equal to height of wall plus 4″ extra for pattern alignment. Make sure print of each panel is straight. Trim down excess leaving a 1″ turn under at top and bottom of each panel. Double check to make sure the panels are equal to the height of the wall (a bit over won't hurt). Press hems in place.

**4.**

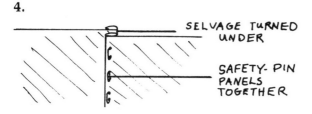

SELVAGE TURNED UNDER

SAFETY-PIN PANELS TOGETHER

When more than one fabric panel is being used, turn selvages under, press them in place, then overlap panels and safety pin them together for easy alignment while fabric is being shirred.

**5.**

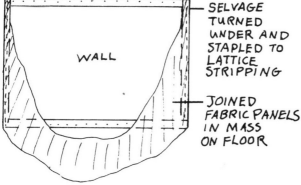

WALL

SELVAGE TURNED UNDER AND STAPLED TO LATTICE STRIPPING

JOINED FABRIC PANELS IN MASS ON FLOOR

To do one wall begin by turning under, pressing in place, then stapling the outermost

selvages of joined fabric panels down opposite sides of wall as illustrated. You will have a mass of fabric flowing onto the floor in the center of your wall area—leave it there for the moment.

**6.**

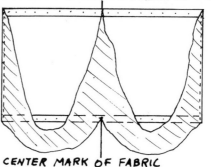

CENTER MARK OF FABRIC STAPLED TO CENTER MARK OF WALL

CENTER MARK OF FABRIC STAPLED TO CENTER MARK OF WALL

Determine the exact center of your wall, top and bottom, and mark. Determine the exact center of your joined fabric panels, top and bottom, and mark. Staple center marks of fabric to center marks of wall. (Put all staples into lattice stripping on the vertical.)

**7.**

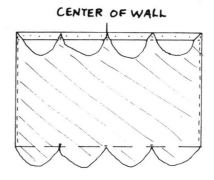

CENTER OF WALL

Determine the exact center of each half of the wall and joined fabric panels, top and bottom, and mark. Staple center marks of fabric to center marks of wall sections. Continue subdividing and stapling on the vertical along top of wall until all fabric is shirred into position (it will look like a lot of tiny tubes). If you have the time, allow fabric to hang for a few hours, then staple bottom of wall area in the same manner as you did the top, being sure to keep panels in alignment (you want shirring on the vertical, not on a slant). Remove all safety pins.

# TEEN-AGE BOY'S ROOM

This is a room designed to feel cozy and warm, and because of its upholstered walls, the noise level is decreased. Simple decorating tricks keep this room in service as a bedroom when "junior" is home from school and as a spare guest room or den when he is away . . . tailored, chic, and easy to care for.

## NO-SEW PROJECTS

*Quilted Mattress Cover and Box Spring Cover*
*Inner Tube Ottoman*
*Leg Casings*
*Fabric-Covered Walls—Upholstered Window Shade with Border Treatment*

mattress covering—measured, marked, and cut so that you have enough fabric to cover top, sides, and 2" to 3" extra to tuck under all

## QUILTED MATTRESS COVER AND BOX SPRING COVER

There are a lot of custom-look tricks to be achieved with the use of ready-mades. No matter what we buy—home furnishings, ready-to-wear, or food—we all like and enjoy instant gratification . . . and this is one of the easiest ways I know to "instantly" gratify a home-furnishings desire.

The best way to create a quilted mattress cover is to purchase a ready-made quilted bedspread or quilted fabric cut to the size of a bedspread. Neatly tuck it in around and under the mattress on all sides.

The box spring cover is a flat sheet or unquilted fabric of the same design as the

QUILTED BEDSPREAD OR QUILTED FABRIC TUCKED UNDER

FLAT SHEET OR FABRIC TUCKED UNDER AND STAPLED OR T-PINNED IN PLACE

MATTRESS

BOX SPRING

the way around. Wrap fabric around the box spring, tuck edges to the underside, and staple in place to the box spring's wooden frame. To give a more professional look, be sure to make neat, squared corners when wrapping the mattress and box spring. This is an ideal look for any active young person's room, or for that matter, anyone's room.

The pillow shams on the bed are purchased. Stuff sleeping pillows inside the shams and you have a twin bed with the look of a custom tailored studio couch.

# INNER TUBE OTTOMAN

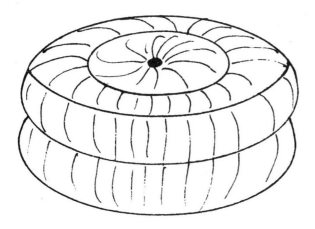

This project is not only fun to make, but twice as much fun to use once completed.

## YOU NEED . . .

**2 truck tire inner tubes** with air valves on insides (usually available at your local garage)
**2 king-size flat sheets** or 19 yards light- to medium-weight fabric, 36″ wide
**Tape measure**
**Marking pencil**
**Fabric shears**
**Iron**

## TO MAKE IT . . .

**1.** Fill inner tubes with air at your local gas station.

**2.** Press fabric flat. Trim off selvages.

**3.** Measure, mark, and cut fabric lengthwise into 6″ or 8″ wide strips. Press raw edges of strips under ¼″ on each long side.

**4.**

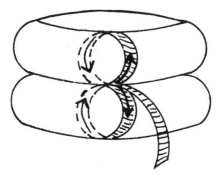

Make a large knot in the end of one strip. Place one inflated inner tube on top of the other. Poke knotted end of fabric strip in between the two tubes. Always keeping strip right side out, begin weaving it around the two tubes in a figure "8", overlapping the strips and pushing them into soft gathers as you do so.

**5.**

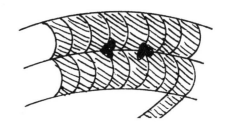

Always begin and end a strip in the center of the tubes. Knot it to a strip and begin weaving again. Continue in this manner until the entire ottoman is covered. You must end with all knots in the center of the tubes. As you weave the fabric strips in and out, give them a yank and the tubes will become pressed more tightly together. Toward the end it will be somewhat difficult to get the strips between the tubes, but persevere—if I can do it, you can do it!

**6.**

To hide all the knots in the center of the ottoman, fill the hole with a pillow and cover it with a scrap of fabric, knotted and fanned. Tuck raw edges down around the pillow.

To turn this ottoman into a low table, top it with a tray or a piece of lucite cut to size.

# LEG CASINGS

This is a wonderful way to camouflage legs on a studio couch or bed and also to add new architectural interest to the basic design.

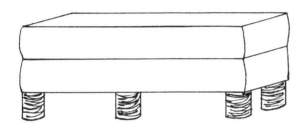

## YOU NEED . . .

**Oatmeal boxes**—economy size, one box per leg to be covered
**Fabric**—1¼ yards medium weight, 48″ wide will cover six legs
**Tape measure**
**Marking pencil**
**Scissors**
**Fabric shears**
**Spray adhesive**
**Iron**

## TO MAKE IT . . .

1.

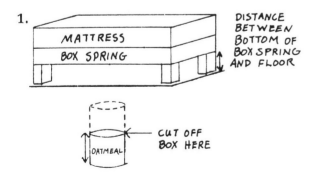

Measure, mark, and cut each oatmeal box at the point that equals the distance between the bottom of the box spring of couch or bed and the floor.

**2.** Press fabric flat. Trim off selvages.

3.

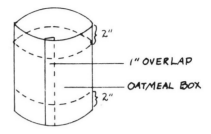

Measure, mark, and cut out sections of fabric, each 4″ longer than the height of each box and 1″ wider than its circumference.

**4.** Working with one at a time, spray adhesive onto outside of oatmeal box. Position fabric so that you have a 2″ overlap at the top and bottom to allow for pattern alignment. Now carefully wrap fabric around box, smoothing it and keeping design straight as you do so.

5.

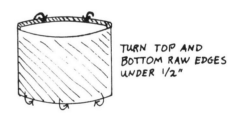

Trim all raw edges down to ½″ overlap. Apply spray adhesive to top inside edge of box and around bottom, and turn raw edges in and under.

**6.** Allow all to dry thoroughly, then set each studio couch or bed leg into its own leg casing.

Try this technique with square or rectangular covered boxes—the result will be very effective.

# FABRIC-COVERED WALLS—UPHOLSTERED

Pushpins
Staple gun and staples
Iron

**TO MAKE IT . . .**

**1.**

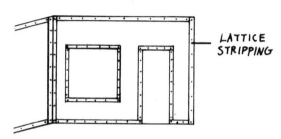

LATTICE STRIPPING

This method is rapidly gaining in popularity as people become more and more energy conservation conscious. Upholstered walls do make a room feel smaller, however. So if you wish to use this method in a small room, do only one wall this way and leave the others unpadded.

*YOU NEED . . .*

**Walls**—can be any color, any texture
**Fabric**—small or large all-over design, random print or stripe, medium-weight
**Wood lattice stripping**—1″ wide by ¼″ thick, enough to go around perimeter of areas to be covered. Don't forget to go around doors, windows, and down both sides of corners (stripping is used as a protection for your walls and can or cannot be used, the choice is yours).
**Polyester quilt batting** or fusible bonding web
**Saw**
**Finishing nails** (headless nails)
**Hammer**
**Chalk**
**String**—as long as wall is high + 12″
**Heavy weight**—to tie to end of string
**Tape measure**
**Marking pencil**
**Fabric shears**

Measure, mark, and cut lattice stripping to proper size, then nail it around perimeter of area to be covered as illustrated.

**2.** To figure how much fabric you need, measure height and width of area to be covered (do not subtract for door or window openings). Add 4″ extra all around to allow for pattern seaming and alignment. If fabric you are using has an obvious repeat, add one extra repeat in length to your requirements.
Press fabric flat. Trim off selvages. Measure, mark, and cut fabric into panels equal to height of wall plus 4″.

**3.**

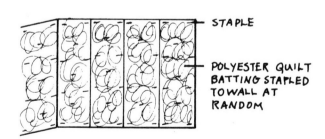

STAPLE

POLYESTER QUILT BATTING STAPLED TO WALL AT RANDOM

Place polyester batting over entire wall surface and hold it in place with staples at random.

**4.**

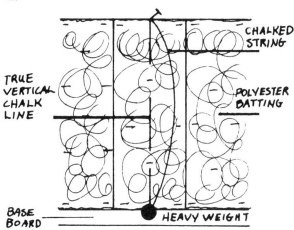

To establish the true vertical line of your wall for positioning fabric correctly, plumb line it. Thumbtack a piece of chalked string to the spot where the ceiling meets the wall and where you will staple your first length of fabric. Tie a heavy weight (rock, washer, hammer, etc.) to the end of the string near the floor to keep it taut. Hold the weight in place with one hand or foot and snap the chalked string with your other hand. If you have kept everything steady, the chalked line on the wall is the true vertical.

**5.** If you are covering a large area and must join fabric panels together, do so at this point with double layers of fusible bonding web cut into ½″ to 1″ wide strips and following manufacturer's directions. Match repeat.

**6.** Handle seamed fabric very gently. Allowing 2″ extra fabric at top of wall area to be covered, begin in a corner and use pushpins to hold fabric to lattice stripping at 6″ intervals. Align fabric design. Trim excess fabric down to ½″.

**7.** If you don't want the staples to show, color their heads to match fabric's background with shoe polish, nail polish, or Magic Marker before dropping them into staple gun.

**8.** Double check to make sure fabric is perfectly aligned. Working out from center of wall toward corners, staple fabric into position across top of walls, turning raw edges under ½″ as you do so, and placing staples

approximately 1″ apart. As you work, gently pull and smooth out wrinkles—do not make the fabric too taut. When stapling fabric down the sides of the walls, try to staple down each simultaneously to keep fabric in alignment. If fabric does not begin and end in a corner, but goes around it, staple down both sides of the corner to keep fabric in alignment and to achieve the proper indentation.

**9.** The last area to be stapled is along the baseboard. If you have inadvertently stretched the fabric, creating an excess while stapling it in place, make tiny tucks all along the baseboard area as you turn raw edges under.

**10.**

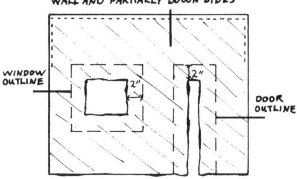

When you have windows and doors to contend with, treat wall area as a giant pumpkin and cut out openings allowing a 2″ excess inside perimeters. After fabric is securely stapled in position across top of wall area, trim away excess, turn raw edges under ½″, and staple in place.

**11.** For a more formally finished effect, attach grosgrain ribbon, braid, or self-welting on top of staples using undiluted white household glue. Random studding with upholsterer's tacks also adds richness to an upholstered wall.

# WINDOW SHADE WITH BORDER TREATMENT

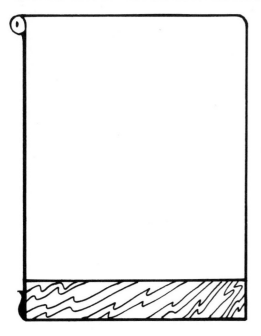

This is a quick and very easy way to enhance a plain white or room-darkening shade. A nice way to complement a room's decor.

## YOU NEED . . .

**Window shade**—white or other color
**Fabric**—with design suitable for use as a border, light- to medium-weight
(If colored shade is being used, fabric should be dark enough not to allow shade to show through.)
**Optional**—printed or plain colored ribbons may be used in place of fabric
**Tape measure**
**Marking pencil**
**Fabric shears**
**Brown wrapping paper**—to catch excess glue
**Spray adhesive**
**Iron**

## TO MAKE IT . . .

**1.** Working with shade right side up, stretch it out on a smooth flat surface. Place heavy books along its edges to keep shade flat.

**2.** Press fabric flat. Trim off selvages. Measure, mark, and cut out the section of fabric you wish to use as a border treatment allowing for 2″ extra to wrap around slat casing to back and ¼″ extra all around for turning raw edges under. Turn and press all raw edges under ¼″, making sure width of fabric is now equal to width of shade.

**3.**

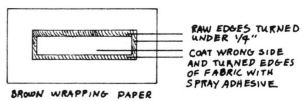

Spread out overlapping sheets of brown wrapping paper on a smooth flat surface. Place fabric border, wrong side up, on top of paper. Coat fabric with spray adhesive and allow it to become a bit tacky.

**4.**

Carefully place fabric along bottom of shade to create a border. Match pressed side edges of fabric to side edges of shade and allow enough excess to wrap around slat casing and onto back of shade (approximately 2″). Carefully smooth out air bubbles with your hands. Allow shade to dry thoroughly before using.

If you wish to enhance the body of your shade with an appliqué and not a border, select and carefully cut out your fabric design, making sure you have no frayed edges. Apply spray adhesive to wrong side of fabric, allow it to become a bit tacky, then carefully smooth it into position on the face of the shade. Allow shade to dry thoroughly before using.

**WARNING**
Continuous rough treatment of shade may cause fabric to pull away from it. If this happens, apply more spray adhesive to fabric and smooth it back into place.

# CHILD'S ROOM

A wonderful place to play, sleep, or entertain is this bright and happily colored room designed with the younger generation in mind. The style is indestructible, yet practical, and oh so easy to live with.

## NO-SEW PROJECTS

*Covered Toy Chest with Appliqué*
*Fabric-Covered Window Shade*
*Mattress Platform Bed*
*Window Shade with Appliqué*
*Wrap and Fan Pillow*

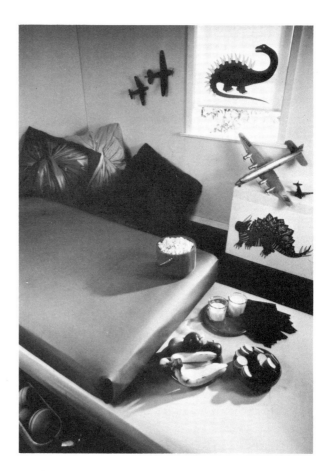

## COVERED TOY CHEST WITH APPLIQUÉ

Everyone should have a toy chest—no matter what age!

Build one out of ¾″ thick plywood (which will make the chest strong enough for sitting upon) to any dimensions you desire. Your local lumberyard can help you. Finish off the chest with a hinged top. Or if you're not handy with the hammer and saw, you may be able to find a nice old wooden chest at a flea market or tag sale.

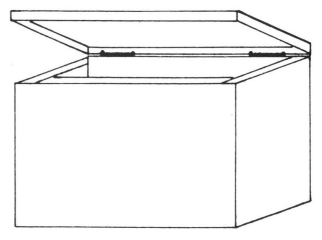

Paint the entire toy chest a flat white inside and out before beginning this project.

## YOU NEED . . .

**Toy chest**—painted flat white
**Fabric**—medium-weight, amount needed depends upon the size of the chest to be covered. You need enough to cover front, sides, and top of chest in one or two pieces of fabric with a 2" turn under.
**Tape measure**
**Marking pencil**
**Fabric shears**
**White household glue**
**Medium-size disposable container**
**Paintbrush**—2" wide
**Steel ruler**
**Single-edge razor blade**
**Clear nail polish**
**Iron**

## TO MAKE IT . . .

**1.** Sand all rough edges.

**2.** Press fabric flat. Trim off selvages.

**3.** Pour white household glue into disposable container and, if necessary, dilute it with a tiny bit of water so that it spreads easily and evenly with a paintbrush.

**4.**

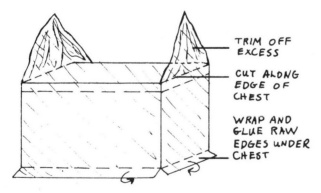

TRIM OFF EXCESS

CUT ALONG EDGE OF CHEST

WRAP AND GLUE RAW EDGES UNDER CHEST

Brush an even coating of glue onto top of toy chest. Center fabric and smooth it into position, making sure you have allowed enough fabric to cover the front of the chest plus 2" extra for turn under.
Brush glue onto front of chest and smooth fabric into position.

**5.** Brush glue onto sides and smooth fabric into place. Cut away excess along top side edges of chest. Wrap and glue raw edges of fabric to back and bottom of toy chest.

**6.**

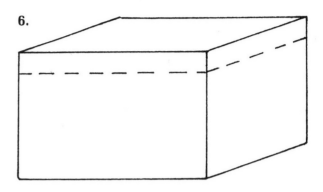

Working with a single-edge razor blade and using a steel ruler as your guide, slit fabric around top of toy chest as illustrated.
Brush all raw fabric edges with clear nail polish to keep them from fraying when in use. A wash of white household glue may also be used for this purpose.

**7.** As a finishing touch to your toy chest, cut out a fabric motif and apply it wherever you wish, using spray adhesive and referring to the directions on page 68 for an appliquéd window shade.

# FABRIC-COVERED WINDOW SHADE

A pretty and easy way to glamorize a "plain jane" window shade, this method works on vinyl, cloth, or paper shades and tends to be exceptionally successful when the fabric's background is a color.

## YOU NEED . . .

**1 window shade**—with roller plus slat, white or off-white, old or new, and clean
**Fabric**—light- to medium-weight and 2" larger than window shade on all sides
**Old sheet**—twin size
**Tape measure**

**Marking pencil**
**Fabric shears**
**Scissors**
**Fusible bonding web**—enough to cover entire face of shade and a bit more
**Masking tape**
**Staple gun and staples**
**Iron**
**Pressing cloth**

## TO MAKE IT . . .

**1.** Press fabric flat. Trim off selvages.

**2.** Spread out old piece of fabric (or an old sheet) on a large flat surface. Unroll shade. Remove it from roller and remove bottom slat.

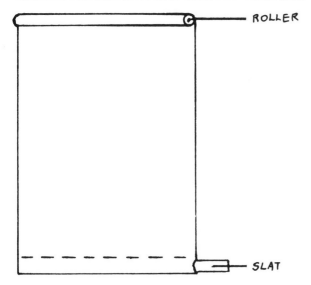

ROLLER

SLAT

**3.**

OLD SHEET TO LAY SHADE ON

RIGHT SIDE OF WINDOW SHADE COVERED WITH FUSIBLE BONDING WEB (FABRIC, RIGHT SIDE UP, IS PLACED ON TOP OF BONDING WEB)

½" EXCESS

3" EXCESS

FUSIBLE BONDING WEB OVERLAPPED ½"

Measure, mark, and cut out (use scissors, bonding web dulls fabric shears) enough

fusible bonding web to cover the entire face of window shade with a ½" excess on the sides and top and 3" excess on the bottom.

Fusible bonding web is purchased in cut-to-length requirements, but is only 18" to 22" wide. Therefore, if the window shade you are covering is wider than 18", overlap lengths of bonding web ½". Don't worry, there will be no "ridge" on the face of your shade because the web melts as it fuses fabric to shade. Measure, mark, and cut out a section of fabric 2" larger than window shade on all sides except the bottom; make that 3" longer.

Place shade, right side up, on top of an old sheet (the sheet is simply to protect your floor or carpet). Place bonding web on the window shade, then very carefully place fabric, right side up, on top of fusible bonding web. Place books around the perimeter of fabric to hold it in place.

Fuse fabric to window shade following manufacturer's directions *except* when covering a vinyl shade. When fusing fabric to a vinyl shade, press (do not iron) fabric and hold iron in place for only 5 seconds. As you fuse fabric to vinyl, the vinyl becomes very soft. After fabric is pressed all over, allow it to dry for about 20 minutes. Repeat pressing procedure two more times, allowing 20 minutes between each pressing. After final pressing allow shade to cool thoroughly.

**4.**

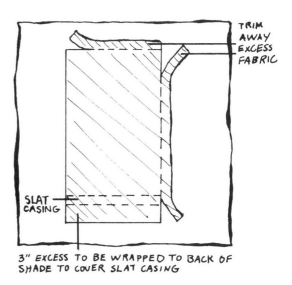

TRIM AWAY EXCESS FABRIC

SLAT CASING

3" EXCESS TO BE WRAPPED TO BACK OF SHADE TO COVER SLAT CASING

Peel shade off of old piece of fabric. Trim away excess fabric from sides and top of shade.

**5.**

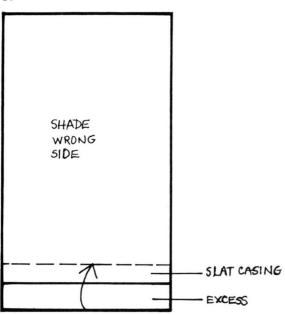

SHADE
WRONG
SIDE

SLAT CASING

EXCESS

Flip shade wrong side up. Trim bottom excess down to depth of slat casing. Measure, mark, and cut out a strip of fusible bonding web equal to excess. Place bonding web on top of slat casing and fold excess up and on top of bonding web. Fuse in place.

**6.** Attach top of shade to roller with masking tape in a reverse roll position. Newer window shades have a guideline on the rollers to make positioning easy. Hang shade in window. Test roll it to make sure shade rolls straight. Remove it from window brackets and securely adhere covered shade to its roller. Staple if roller is cardboard, tape if roller is metal.

# MATTRESS PLATFORM BED

A fun and inexpensive way to create a lot of sleeping area for an "entertaining" child is to fill the room with mattresses. Create artistic platform arrangements, stack them, or spread them out flat. Cover with fitted sheets and you have a colorful, comfortable area for your energetic tiny tot to play in, sleep in, and have slumber parties in.

# WINDOW SHADE WITH APPLIQUÉ

An ordinary plain white cloth or vinyl window shade can be easily transformed into an integral part of your room's decorating scheme.

Select a fabric motif applicable to the room's decor. Using fabric shears, cut it out very carefully.

Lay your window shade out, right side up, on a large smooth surface.

Lay fabric cutout, wrong side up, on a flat surface covered with brown wrapping paper. Apply spray adhesive to fabric, allow it to become a bit tacky, then carefully position and smooth the motif into place where you want it on the window shade.

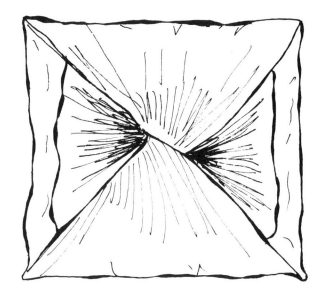

# WRAP AND FAN PILLOW

To me, this is one of the most beautiful projects in this book.

For the photograph we made this pillow by following the basic directions for the Wrap and Tie Pillow on page 34. But cut your fabric to be more of a rectangle than a square and position the pillow parallel to the fabric. Fold the two opposite sides of fabric over edges of pillow as illustrated. Tie remaining opposite sides of fabric together. Fan out ties and fold raw edges under so that the fans do not extend beyond the edges of the pillow. If fans flop, use a few strategically placed dressmaker pins to hold them in position.

For more practical purposes and especially for use in a child's room, follow the basic directions for the Wrap and Tie Pillow but use an extra large section of fabric to do so. The extra long ends will then be easy to shape into a fan effect.

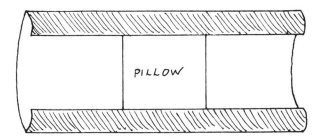

PILLOW

# SINGLE PROJECTS

*The following pages contain directions for additional individual no-sew items which can be used in various rooms throughout your home. They range from practical to fun to hard to easy to fast to slow . . . and they are all wonderful no-sew projects.*

## BRUSHED DENIM PLACE MATS

Brushed denim (or any other washable fabric) pressed onto nonwoven fusible backing for home decorating is a quick, easy way to create an impressive hostess gift.

### YOU NEED . . .

For six place mats:
**Fabric**—1 yard light- to medium weight, 42" wide, washable
**Nonwoven fusible backing**—for home decorating
**Nonwoven fusible bonding web**
**Tape measure**
Marking pencil
Fabric shears
Scissors

### TO MAKE IT . . .

**1.** Place mats usually measure approximately 12" × 18" (place mats shown here are actually 11" × 18"). Therefore, to make one mat, measure, mark, and cut out a section of fabric and fusible backing, each 14" × 20". Follow manufacturer's directions for application.

**2.** Pink all raw edges, then turn them under to create a mat approximately 12" × 18", or a bit smaller.

**3.**

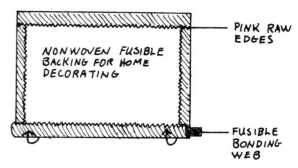

Measure, mark, and cut out four strips of fusible bonding web (use scissors) the same size as each of the turned under edges. Fuse raw edges into position following manufacturer's directions.

**4.** Measure, mark, and cut a 1½" wide slit on left-hand side of place mat to hold a napkin. (Bandanas make fantastic napkins and are especially compatible with brushed denim place mats.)

# BOTANICAL PLACE MATS

Fruit or floral motifs in a fabric within their own rectangles or squares offer an instant place mat idea.

Working on a smooth flat surface covered with brown wrapping paper, cut fabric squares apart, lay them on ⅛″ thick cork cut to size, and apply ten coats of acrylic sealer to face of fabric. Allow to dry 20 minutes between each application.

# CORK-BACKED PLACE MATS

These can be made in any shape you desire—animals, shells, flowers, and so on. This is also a nice gift for that special child in your life—make a place mat, then a bib to match with the leftover scraps.

## YOU NEED . . .

**Fabric**—medium-weight with motifs large enough to be place mats
**Sheets of cork**—⅛″ thick, and enough to back fabric motifs
**Spray paint**—flat white
**Plastic drop cloth**
**Fabric shears**
**Acrylic sealer**
**Sponge paintbrush**
**Mat knife**
**Clear varnish**
**Paintbrush**—2″ wide
**Iron**

## TO MAKE IT . . .

**1.** Spray-paint cork a flat white and allow to dry thoroughly before continuing.

**2.** Press fabric flat. Trim off selvages.

**3.** Roughly cut out fabric motifs and place them on top of painted sheets of cork. Working on top of a plastic drop cloth, secure them in place on cork with one coat of acrylic sealer applied to a sponge paintbrush. Allow to dry thoroughly. Now apply at least ten more coats of acrylic sealer, brushing in alternating horizontal and vertical directions. Allow a minimum 30-minute drying period between each application.

**4.**

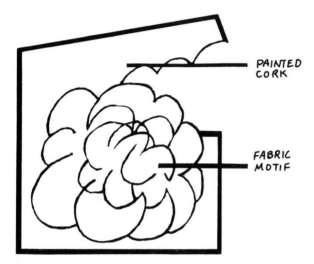

PAINTED CORK

FABRIC MOTIF

When sealer is thoroughly dry, use a mat knife to cut around each cork-backed motif.

**5.** A protective coat of clear vanish should be applied to all mats before they are used.

# DISHCLOTH PLACE MATS

Dishcloths pressed onto nonwoven fusible backing are quickly transformed into cheery place mats to use for picnics or for informal dining. Follow manufacturer's directions for application.

Use additional dishcloths as napkins.

# TRIVETS

One never has enough trivets—at least I never do. This is an easy way to create as many attractive ones as you need. When they are not in use as trivets, they can be hung on your kitchen walls.

## YOU NEED . . .

**Wooden picture frames**—with flat surfaces, in assorted sizes to accommodate platters and casseroles
**Fabric**—sections with motifs able to be centered in frames
**1 sheet foam-core board**
**Steel ruler**
**Marking pencil**
**Mat knife**
**Fabric shears**
**Plastic drop cloth**
**Acrylic sealer**
**Sponge paintbrush**
**Clear varnish**
**Paintbrush**—2″ wide
**Staple gun and staples**
**Iron**

## TO MAKE IT . . .

**1.** Paint or stain picture frames to compliment your fabric motifs.

**2.** Measure, mark, and cut out sections of foam-core board (with a mat knife) to fit into each frame.

**3.**

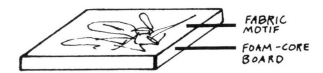

Measure, mark, and cut out fabric motifs the exact size of each section of foam-core board.

**4.** Working with right sides up and on top of plastic drop cloth, place fabric on top of foam-core board. Using a sponge paintbrush, apply one coat of acrylic sealer to the face of the fabric. Allow to dry thoroughly.

**5.** Now apply at least ten more coats of acrylic sealer in alternating horizontal and vertical directions with each coat. Allow a minimum 30-minute drying period between each application.

**6.** Apply a protective coat of clear varnish to face of fabric. Allow to dry thoroughly.

**7.**

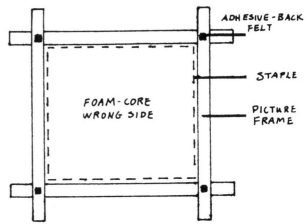

Staple foam-core section to back of picture frame.
Attach adhesive-backed felt to corners of wrong side of picture frame to prevent it from scratching your table.

# BORDER-TRIMMED MIRROR

A shiny metal frame from the five-and-ten, a paper picture mat from the art supply store, an inexpensive piece of mirror cut to fit, and a few scraps of fabric are all you need to create this charming border-trimmed mirror. (This is also an extra special way to frame a picture.) Select a white picture mat with an interesting center shape (oval, round, rectangle, etc.). Cover the entire mat's face with a piece of solid color fabric and secure it in position with spray adhesive.

Cut out the center of your fabric-covered mat following the mat's center shape, allowing 1″ overlap around inner edges. Notch raw edges and turn them to back of mat.

Wrap outer edges of fabric around to back of mat, and trim away excess at corners to create a flat, mitered effect. Use spray adhesive to hold fabric in place on wrong side of mat.

Place fabric-covered mat in frame, and slide mirror into frame behind mat. Now select and cut out your favorite motif in assorted sizes—flowers, fruits, vegetables, animals, shells, or whatever you want. Lay cutouts on waxed paper and using a sponge paintbrush apply four coats of acrylic sealer to them. Allow 20 to 30 minutes for drying between each application.

Position cutouts around mirror on fabric border and secure them in place with spray adhesive.

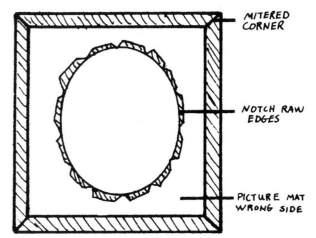

MITERED CORNER

NOTCH RAW EDGES

PICTURE MAT WRONG SIDE

# FRAMED FABRIC

Framing a fabric motif is done the same way you frame a towel. Select a pretty scene. Staple fabric to a stretcher bar frame (see page 15 for basic directions). Take the stretched fabric to a frame-it-yourself shop and select a frame you like.

# REVERSIBLE CURTAINS

These are as pretty from the outside looking in as they are from the inside looking out. Each curtain panel is made of lightweight fabrics, a solid color and a print, and is held

together with double layers of fusible bonding web. Because this is a fragile way of making curtains, your gathering should be shallow.

Working on a smooth flat surface and with one panel (right side up) at a time, lay double layers of ½" wide fusible bonding web strips around outer edge of solid color fabric panel as illustrated. Make sure that the strips do not go beyond areas to be used for rod casing and ½″ hem allowance at top of panel.

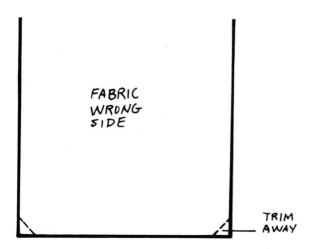

FABRIC WRONG SIDE

TRIM AWAY

*Carefully* place right side of print panel on top of right side of solid color panel. Fuse the two fabric sections together following manufacturer's directions. Trim away excess from fused corners and turn curtain panel right side out. Press.

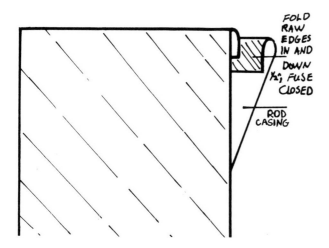

FOLD RAW EDGES IN AND DOWN ½; FUSE CLOSED

ROD CASING

Fold top raw edges of curtain panel in and down ½″. Press. Fuse ½″ seam allowance together with two layers of fusible bonding web. Repeat above steps to make second curtain panel. Carefully thread fabric panels onto curtain rod and arrange gathers.

Use pushpins to hold curtain panels away from window showing their reverse sides. Arrange fabric so that pushpins are hidden.

# FRAMED TOWEL

There are many towels designed and sold today pretty enough to be a picture. Therefore, why not do it! Purchase a pretty-as-a-picture towel—any size. A frame-it-yourself store can help you stretch the towel and select a frame that will complement the design. The nicest thing about framing a towel is that when you are tired of using it as a picture, you can unframe it and put it to use for the purpose for which it was intended.

# COVERED STEPLADDER

A good way to dress up a utilitarian kitchen item, such as your basic wooden stepladder, is to cover it with a bright cheerful fabric and bring it into your room decorating scheme.

Make sure your stepladder is painted a flat white. Then, using white household glue, cut, wrap, and adhere fabric to stepladder beginning with the legs first, top second, and the steps last.

# BANDANA CUSHIONED STOOL

This is an easy way to add color and comfort to a plain, hard wooden stool. Pad top of wooden stool with a piece of foam rubber (½″ to 1″ thick) cut to size. Place a bandana square over foam and tie each corner of fabric to a leg of the stool with a contrasting colored ribbon.

# WASTEBASKET

This is a beautiful room accessory whether used as a wastebasket or to house potted plants. Depending upon the type of fabric and tie closures used, this project can be young, sophisticated, feminine, or very masculine.

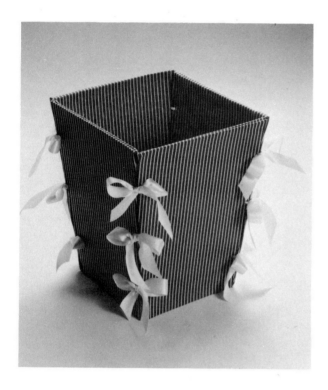

## YOU NEED . . .

**White cardboard**—heavyweight
**Fabric**—light- to medium weight
**Tape measure**
**Marking pencil**
**Fabric shears**
**Mat knife**
**Ice pick**
**White household glue**
**Small disposable container**
**Paintbrush**—2″ wide
**Thread and needle**
**Satin ribbon**—1″ wide and cut into twelve 18″ long pieces
**Heavy books**
**Iron**

## TO MAKE IT . . .

1.

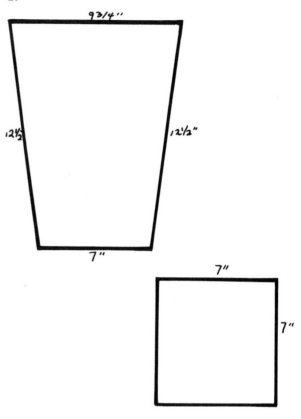

Measure, mark, and cut out eight cardboard sides as illustrated.
Measure, mark, and cut out two cardboard sides as illustrated.

2. Measure, mark, and cut out eight fabric sections, each equal to a cardboard side + 1″ extra all around. Measure, mark, and cut out two fabric sections equal to cardboard bottoms + 1″ extra all around.

3. Pour white household glue into disposable container and, if necessary, dilute with a tiny bit of water so that it spreads easily and evenly with a paintbrush.

4. Working with one at a time, brush glue onto the face of a cardboard side. Allow to become a bit tacky. Center fabric over face, right side up, and smooth it into position. Wrap and glue raw edges to wrong side of cardboard. Repeat this procedure for all eight cardboard sections

plus the two bottom sections. Allow all to dry thoroughly.

**5.**

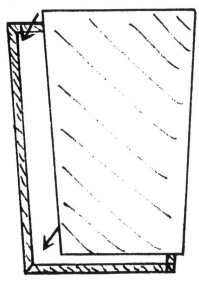

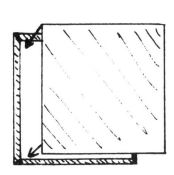

Glue wrong sides of all fabric-covered cardboard sections together creating a total of four sides and one bottom. Place heavy books on top of each section and allow to dry thoroughly.

**6.**

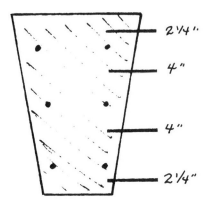

2¼"

4"

4"

2¼"

Using an ice pick, punch holes along the length of each cardboard side as illustrated.

**7.**

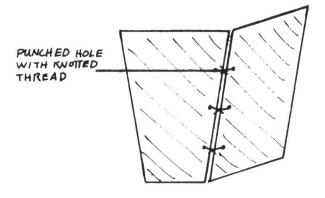

PUNCHED HOLE
WITH KNOTTED
THREAD

Join sides together by pulling a double threaded needle through the punched holes. Knot thread.

**8.**

Push a strip of ribbon through each hole with ice pick. Tie ribbons into bows.

**9.** The wastebasket bottom may remain loose or be attached to one side of basket with thread pushed through holes. The bottom, pushed into position, will maintain the basket's shape.

# COVERED GARBAGE PAIL

This is a cheery way to disguise a large garbage can for in-house use. Put it in the kitchen for rubbish, in a child's room for toys, or in your own bedroom to hold soiled laundry.

## YOU NEED . . .

**Metal garbage pail**—any size
**Fabric**—enough to go around can and to cover lid, solid color, light- to medium-weight
**Tape measure**
**Marking pencil**
**Spray adhesive**
**Large safety pin**

If you are using a light-colored fabric, paint garbage pail and lid a flat white before beginning this project.

## TO MAKE IT . . .

1. Paint garbage pail handles on sides and on lid, plus rims, with a high gloss, in a color that is compatible with the fabric you're using.

2. Press fabric flat. Cut off selvages.

3. Measure, mark, and cut out a section of fabric large enough to wrap around the body of the garbage pail.

4. Apply spray adhesive to pail, one quarter section at a time. Wrap fabric around pail—overlap seam edges ¼" and ease and tuck top and bottom raw edges of fabric underneath rims of pail with the help of a large safety pin.

5.

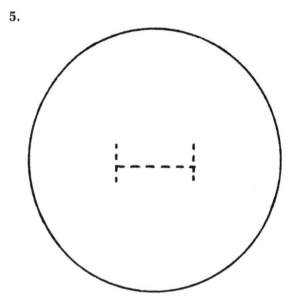

Measure, mark, and cut out a circle of fabric large enough to cover garbage pail lid. Place fabric on top of lid. Carefully mark, then cut slits in circle where handle will fit through.

6. Apply spray adhesive to lid and cover lid with fabric, allowing handle to come through slits. Ease and tuck raw edges into rim of lid with the help of a large safety pin.

# DIRECTOR'S CHAIR COVER

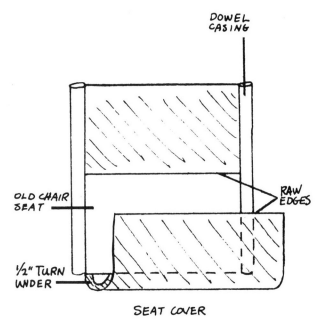

facturer's directions, fuse and wrap fabric around chair's back cover and around seat cover as illustrated. Remember to turn all raw edges under except where seams are formed. Do not allow seat covering to extend beyond the dowel casing stitches of the original seat.

An easy way to give a faded or badly stained director's chair cover a new look is to camouflage it. Medium-weight fabric plus fusible bonding web are all you need. Measure the length and width of back cover and seat cover, add ½" around all sides of each, and multiply each final measure by 2.

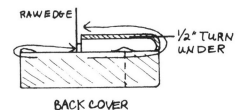

Measure, mark, and cut out fabric plus fusible bonding web to match measures of chair covers plus ½" turn under. Following manu-

# COVERED BOLSTERS

Covered foam bolsters are a wonderful and inexpensive way to add decorative character to an otherwise boring studio couch.

To cover a bolster 37″ long and 25½″ in circumference and 8″ in diameter, one bath towel, approximately 27″ × 49″ is just perfect (or use 1⅔ yards of 36″ wide fabric). Toweling is a soft, absorbent, and easy-to-care-for covering for bolsters, especially if they are to be moved much or used for on-the-floor lounging.

Place bolster in center of bath towel on the vertical. Wrap towel around bolster and secure it in place with T-pins.

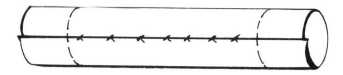

Working with one end at a time, hold bolster upright between your knees, turn end under,

and fold into center, butting edges of towel as illustrated.

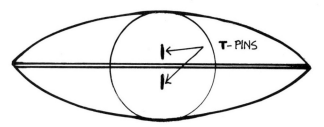

Fold in two opposite sides and T-pin in place. Now make folds in remaining areas and T-pin to hold in position. You should have eight T-pins in each end of bolster.

Do not use this covering technique for children's areas. The pins go in tightly, but one might slip out if the bolster gets very active handling.

# BOLSTER HEADBOARD—HORIZONTAL

This type of headboard can be easily constructed in less than an hour from towel-covered foam bolsters. They are ideal for comfort and easy care. See page 82 for basic Covered Bolsters directions.

For a twin-size headboard lay three covered bolsters on a smooth flat surface. For a larger than twin-size headboard just work with more bolsters to achieve the width you desire.

Beginning with the bottom bolster, wrap 1½" to 2" wide ribbon around one end securing it to the bolster above in a figure eight fashion. (If you wish, extra strips of ribbon can be separately wrapped around bolsters to create a design.) Secure ribbon in position at back of bolsters with T-pins. Leave two long ends on ribbon. Repeat same procedure for opposite ends of bolsters. Beginning at mattress level, position bolsters directly behind head of bed. Nail ribbon ends to wall, allowing bolsters to hang free. Make a perky bow for each side of bolster headboard and nail it in place over raw ribbon ends.

# BOLSTER HEADBOARD—VERTICAL

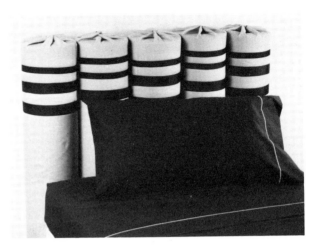

This vertical bolster headboard is not only super-easy to make, but can be enlarged to any width needed by the simple addition of more bolsters. Five covered and embellished foam bolsters are needed to create a twin-size headboard.

Each bolster is covered separately following the basic Covered Bolsters directions on page 82. Each is then embellished with ribbon stripes, strips of ribbon cut to size, wrapped around each bolster separately, and T-pinned into position.

Line up the covered bolsters on the floor behind the head of the bed and secure each to the wall with a pushpin or headless nail.

# GATHERED LAMPSHADE

This is an easy way to add a fresh, feminine look to a stocky lamp base without spending excessive dollars for a new shade.

Measure, mark, and cut fabric as follows:

Width = 2 times bottom circumference of shade

Length = height of shade + 2″

Fold top raw edge of fabric down 1″. Fuse in place with ¾″ long strips of fusible bonding web which are as wide as the fabric you are working with. Fuse bonding web along bottom raw edge to create a ¼″ wide top casing. Thread casing with package string.

Overlap back seam ½″ and fuse in place.

Place fabric over lampshade and gently gather it in until it rests on rim of shade. Knot string securely at this point.

Measure and mark where hem should be. Fold raw edge under and fuse in place with strips of bonding web.

# FABRIC TUBE FLOOR LAMP

Making your own floor or table lamp is not as difficult as you may imagine, and the savings in dollars are well worth your time and effort. To do this project a discarded fabric tube was used. Heavyweight fabric tubes can usually be obtained free from your local fabric store.

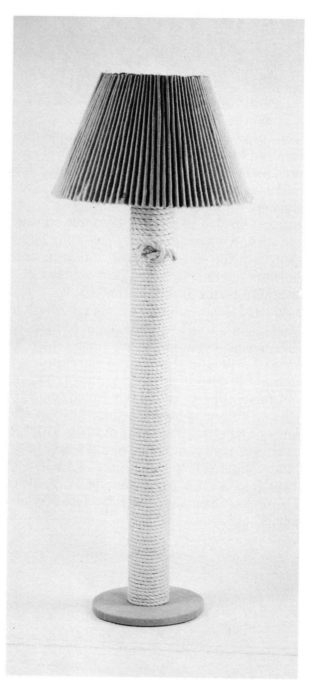

## YOU NEED . . .

**1 cardboard fabric tube**—46″ long, 3½″ in diameter, and ¼″ to ½″ thick
**45 yards sisal rope**—½″ thick
**Plywood**—½″ thick and cut into a 10″ disc
**Burlap**—enough to cover disc and lampshade
**Plastic drop cloth**
**Saw**
**Wood glue**
**Spray adhesive**
**Drill**
**Nails**
**Hammer**
**1 lamp parts repair kit**
**Pleated lampshade**—12½″ high with a bottom diameter of 20″

If fabric tube is not the height you need, measure, mark, and saw it down to height suggested above or to the height you desire.

## TO MAKE IT . . .

**1.**

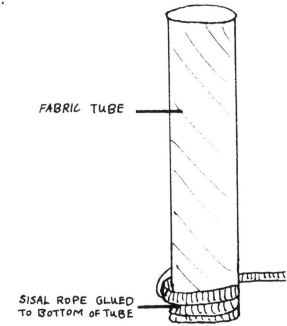

FABRIC TUBE

SISAL ROPE GLUED TO BOTTOM OF TUBE

Cover floor with plastic drop cloth.
Using wood glue, anchor one end of sisal rope to bottom of fabric tube.
Hold rope in place while glue dries.

**2.**

Doing a small section at a time, apply spray adhesive to tube, then wrap rope around tube. Continue spraying and wrapping until entire tube is covered. If you must piece rope, do so by knotting it and incorporating the knot into the design. End rope as you began it, by securing it in position with wood glue.

**3.** Adhere a section of burlap to plywood disc with spray adhesive. Wrap and glue raw edges to underside of disc.

**4.**

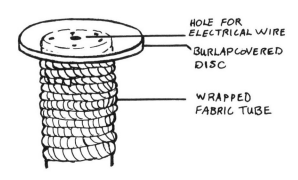

HOLE FOR ELECTRICAL WIRE

BURLAP COVERED DISC

WRAPPED FABRIC TUBE

Drill a hole in center of disc.
Nail covered disc to wrapped fabric tube.

**5.** Thread lamp wire down through sisal wrapped tube and through base. Secure lamp parts to top of tube following manufacturer's directions.

**6.** To complete your lamp, cover pleated lampshade with burlap following the directions on page 52.

## DRAPED AND GATHERED LAMPSHADE

This is a way to hide an old or ugly A-line lampshade and create a romantic effect. Measure, mark, and cut out fabric squares half again as long as the height of the shade. Turn squares on the diagonal and drape them over the top of shade so that a corner point hangs below lower rim of shade about 2″ (experi-

ment and trim squares down if necessary). Use doubled-face tape to hold opposite corner point of fabric in place on wrong side of shade. Gently arrange squares into soft gathers as you place them around shade.

## WRAPPED AND GATHERED LAMPSHADE

A quick way to redo a drum-styled silk lampshade. Remove the old silk from shade frame. Measure, mark, and cut fabric into 5¼″ wide strips, turn raw edges under ¼″, and press in place. Wrap strips around frame, gathering them slightly as you go. Use dressmaker's pins to join strips together on wrong side of shade as you are wrapping. Make sure the fabric never comes in contact with the light bulb.

# FABRIC-COVERED SQUARE BOXES

This is an easy, attractive way to give your closets or storage areas a fresh new look. This is also a pretty and practical way to wrap presents for any occasion.

## YOU NEED . . .

For one box 8½" square × 5" deep:
**Fabric**—1 yard medium weight, 44" wide
**Tape measure**
**Marking pencil**
**Fabric shears**
**White household glue**
**Small disposable container**
**Paintbrush**—1½" wide
**Optional Trim**—1 yard braid, ½" wide in accent color, or 1 yard bias-covered cord in accent color

## TO MAKE IT . . .

**1.** Press fabric flat. Trim off selvages.
Make sure box you are covering is white or off-white. If it is not, apply flat white paint to outside of box and its top. Allow it to dry thoroughly before you begin.

**2.**

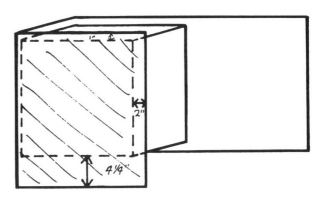

Measure, mark, and cut out a strip of fabric wide enough to wrap around box bottom with a 2" overlap, and long enough to have a 1" turn under at top and a 4¼" turn under on the bottom (approximately 36½" × 11").

**3.** Pour white household glue into disposable container and, if necessary, dilute it with a tiny bit of water so that glue spreads easily and evenly with a paintbrush.

**4.** Brush an even coating of glue onto one side of box. Beginning at corner edge, smooth fabric into position, right side out, allowing fabric to extend beyond box 1" at the top and 4¼" at the bottom. Make sure fabric is aligned properly and continue gluing it into position around box.

**5.**

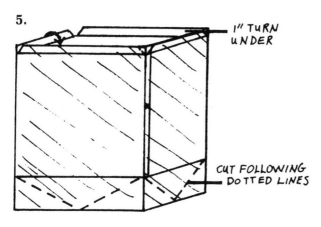

1" TURN UNDER

CUT FOLLOWING DOTTED LINES

Trim excess down to ¼" along side corner of box, turn raw edges under and glue in place. Trim out a notch from each corner around top to enable fabric to lay flat. Brush glue around inside top of box and fold in excess.

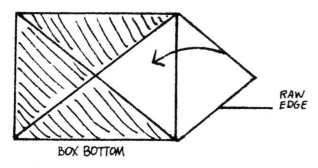

RAW EDGE

BOX BOTTOM

**6.** Measure, mark, and cut fabric overlap for box bottom into triangles so that raw edges butt together and form an "X". Glue triangles into position. Allow to dry thoroughly.

**7.** From remaining fabric, measure, mark, and cut out a square large enough to cover box top with a ½" overlap (approximately 13" × 13").

**8.**

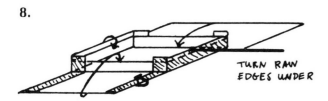

TURN RAW EDGES UNDER

Brush glue onto lid top, then center and smooth fabric into position. Glue sides into place on two opposite sides of lid allowing excess at corners to stay free. Cut as illustrated. Wrap and glue raw edges around corners and to inside of lid.

**9.** Fold in raw edges on remaining two sides and glue in place (if folded raw edges appear to be a bit bulky, gently press bulk down with a hot iron).

**10.** Optional—using undiluted glue, attach braid to outer sides of lid and covered cording to inside of lid so that it extends a little beyond as an accent.

# FABRIC TUBE TABLE

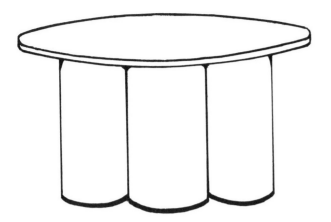

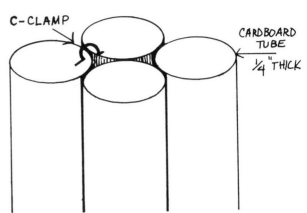

the table, the more tubes you will need for a center base.

This is a fun project with many possibilities. Fabric tubes can usually be obtained free of charge from your local fabric store. They are what manufacturers use to roll and ship fabric on, to keep it from being wrinkled during shipping and storing.

## YOU NEED . . .

**Plywood**—½″ thick, cut to size of top you desire
**Fabric tubes**—¼″ thick and cut to height you desire
**Fabric**—medium weight and enough to cover table's top and tube base
**Wood glue**
**C-clamps**
**Fabric shears**
**Tape measure**
**Marking pencil**
**Spray paint**—flat white
**White household glue**
**Small disposable container**
**Paintbrush**—2″ wide
**Saw**
**Iron**
**Broom closet screw clamp**

## TO MAKE IT . . .

**1.** Decide upon the height and size of your table and saw tubes accordingly. The larger

To create center base, secure tubes together with wood glue, then hold them in position with C-clamps until dry. (If you are making a thick base for a large tabletop, you will have to glue the tubes together in small sections.)

**2.** When tube base is dry, spray paint it flat white and allow it to dry thoroughly.

**3.** Press fabric flat. Trim off selvages. Measure, mark, and cut out a section of fabric large enough to cover table base with an excess of 1″ at top and bottom.

**4.** Pour white household glue into disposable container, and if necessary, dilute with a tiny bit of water so that it spreads easily and evenly with a paintbrush.

**5.** Brush glue onto table base and wrap fabric around it, right side out. Be sure to push fabric into indentations (use dull edge of fabric shears) where tubes meet and to tuck top and bottom raw edges under. Glue these edges in place as well.

**6.** Measure, mark, and cut tabletop to desired size. Spray paint it flat white and allow it to dry thoroughly.

**7.** Cover tabletop with fabric the same way you covered the tube base. Wrap and glue raw edges in place to underside of the tabletop.

**8.**

BROOM CLOSET SCREW CLAMP

Attach a broom closet screw clamp to the center of tabletop. Clamp tabletop onto tube base. If top wobbles, place small wood or cardboard wedges between base and top for stabilization.

# FABRIC TUBE BOOKCASE

Whether used to create lamps, tables, bookcases, or to add architectural interest to a room, fabric tubes offer an inexpensive way to create new dimensions in decorating.

Bookcases are a popular necessity for any living situation and are relatively simple to make with ¼" thick fabric tubes, which are usually throwaways from your local fabric store.

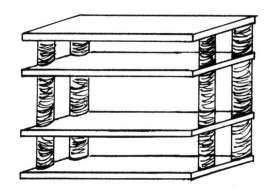

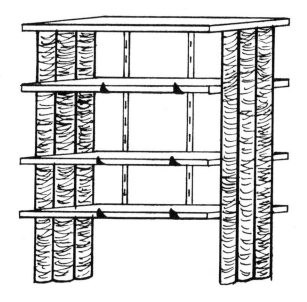

Plywood, a saw, wood glue, hammer, nails, a bit of paint, and some fabric are all you need. The styles you devise are limited only by your own imagination.

# ROOM AND DOOR BORDERS

Room and door borders are easy to do with ribbons, gimp, or fabric. This is a nice way to add architectural interest to a room without feeling that you're stuck with it forever once you do it. Select your design, ribbon, or braid. Decide where you want it, then apply it with undiluted white household glue or spray adhesive.

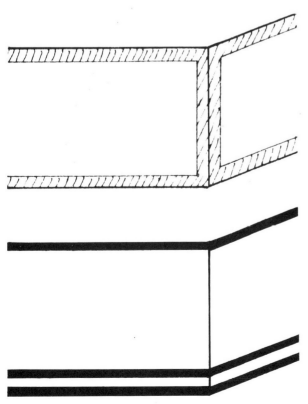

# LUGGAGE RACK STRAPS

Anyone who entertains and has overnight guests should own a luggage rack. Whether for luggage or with a bedside tray, it is a practical decoration for any guest room or guest area. Try to pick one up at a flea market. Simply give it a fresh coat of paint or stain and add some smart new straps of ribbon, braid, or fabric. Now you have added yet another gracious touch to your reputation for thoughtful hospitality.

## YOU NEED . . .

**Fabric**—½ yard medium- to heavyweight, or ribbon or braid approximately 2½″ wide and 19″ long
**Tape measure**
**Marking pencil**
**Fabric shears**
**Scissors**
**Fusible bonding web**
**Staple gun and staples**
**Iron**

## TO MAKE IT . . .

**1.** Press fabric flat. Trim off selvages.

**2.** Measure, mark, and cut out three strips of fabric, each 6″ × 19″.

**3.** On each strip turn all raw edges under ¼″ and press. Measure, mark, and cut out (use scissors, the bonding web will dull your fabric shears) 16 strips of fusible bonding web, each ¼″ wide and as long as each strip. Fuse raw edges in place following manufacturer's directions.

**4.**

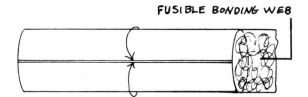

FUSIBLE BONDING WEB

Fold each strip lengthwise, right sides out, with edges meeting in the center of one side. Measure, mark, and cut out three strips of bonding web, the width and length of each folded fabric strip. Place bonding web inside each strip and fuse fabric together following manufacturer's directions.

**5.** Evenly space, then staple the fabric, ribbon, or braid straps to underside of luggage rack.

# GATHERED HEADBOARD

This is an easy way to transform a plain "slab" of a bed into one with dramatic character.

## YOU NEED . . .

**Plywood**—½″ thick and cut to size
**Fabric**—medium- to heavyweight, 2 to 2½ times the width of bed and once again as long, or sheeting double the size of the bed
**Polyester batting**—enough to cover the plywood twice
**Newspaper**
**Cellophane tape**
**Tape measure**
**Marking pencil**
**Scissors**
**Fabric shears**
**T-pins**
**Staple gun and staples**
**Hammer**
**Headless nails**
**Iron**

## TO MAKE IT . . .

**1.** Draw and cut out an outline of a dome headboard from taped-together sheets of newspaper. Your outline should be 1″ wider than bed's mattress width and as high from the floor as you wish (36″ to 49″ is usually a good height).

Take the newspaper pattern to your local lumberyard and have them cut out the shape in ½″ thick plywood.

**2.**

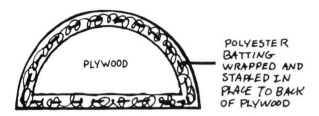

PLYWOOD

POLYESTER BATTING WRAPPED AND STAPLED IN PLACE TO BACK OF PLYWOOD

Wrap and staple two layers of polyester batting over front and around to wrong side of plywood as illustrated.

**3.**

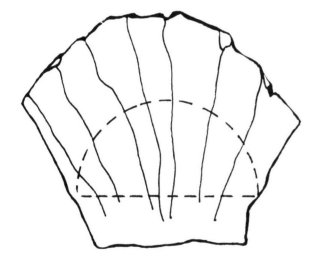

Lay headboard flat on the floor, right side up, and arrange fabric, right side up, in gathers along base of headboard so that it fans out at the top. (If you are working with two sections of fabric, fold raw edges under and into gathers.) Hold fabric gathers in place with T-pins and tuck raw edges under. Carefully turn headboard to other side and staple fabric gathers in place.

**4.** Lean or nail finished headboard against wall behind head of bed.

# DRAPED BED CANOPY

Drape fabric over a hanging plant holder, centered over head of bed. Tie sides back with ribbons, and tack to wall. Or drape fabric over tiebacks.

# GATHERED BED CANOPIES

A canopy bed needn't be a four-poster. You can create a beautiful half crown or rectangle-type canopy for any size bed all by yourself with a section of plywood, a few nails, and your favorite fabric or sheets.

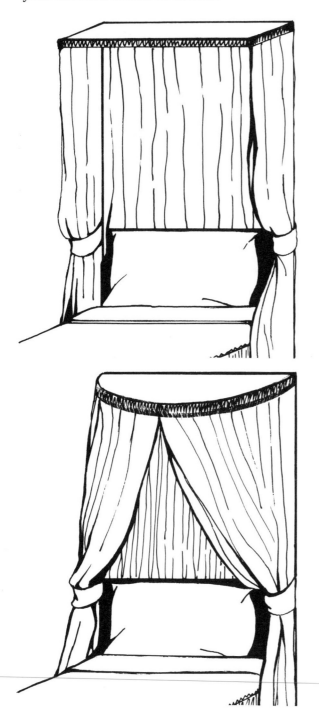

**Plywood**—½" thick disc or rectangle cut to the size you desire. Suggestion: diameter of disc = one-half the width of your bed; rectangle = width of your bed × depth of your pillow or 14"
**Fabric**—light- to medium weight, enough to cover disc or rectangle and to create floor-to-ceiling gathered side panels and a gathered back panel for rectangle (sheets are excellent for this project)
**Tape measure**
**Marking pencil**
**Fabric shears**
**Scissors**
**Pushpins**
**Fusible bonding web**
**Hammer**
**Brads** (headless nails)
**Staple gun and staples**
**Iron**
**Optional trim:** Ribbon, ½" wide and enough to go around edge of canopy

**1.**

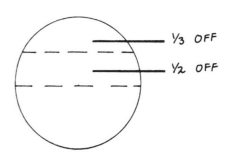

⅓ OFF
½ OFF

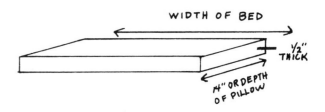

WIDTH OF BED
½" THICK
14" OR DEPTH OF PILLOW

To create a crownlike effect with your plywood disc, measure, mark, and cut out a circle the size you desire (or make a disc with its diameter equal to one-half the width of your bed). Cut off one-third or one-half of the disc to create a flat side to be put against the line where ceiling meets wall. If you are working with a rectangle, measure, mark, and cut it to equal the width of your bed and 14" deep or to equal the depth of your pillow.

**2.** Press fabric flat. Trim off selvages.
Measure, mark, and cut out a section of fabric large enough to cover plywood disc or rectangle plus 1½" extra all around. Place fabric, right side up, on top of disc or rectangle. Pull raw edges to reverse side of wood and staple in place.

**3.** For canopy sides measure, mark, and cut out two sections of fabric, each measuring as follows:
length = floor to ceiling plus 7"
width for disc = 2½ times one-half the circumference
width for rectangle = 2½ times the depth

**4.** For canopy back:
For disc, cover wall behind your bed following directions for shirred, pasted, or stapled walls found throughout this book.
For rectangle, measure, mark, and cut out a section of fabric as follows:
length = floor to ceiling plus 7"
width = 2½ times the width of your bed.
(The rectangle canopy's back can also be a covered wall technique of your choice found throughout the pages of this book.)

**5.** Turn down all top raw edges 1" and press. Set all fabric sections aside.

**6.** Now center and nail covered disc or rectangle to ceiling above the head of your bed.

**7.** Test hang a canopy side section by push-pinning it into the side edge of disc or rectangle. Mark for hem. Remove fabric. Turn up all side sections to make a 5" hem with a 1" turn under. Press in place. Using scissors, measure, mark, and cut out fusible bonding web strips 1" long and as wide as each panel of fabric you are working with. Fuse hems in place following manufacturer's directions.

**8.**

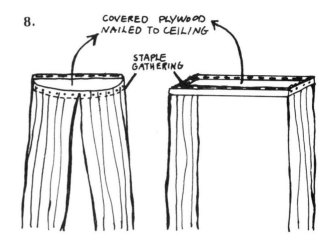

Staple-gather side panels to disc or rectangle edges on the vertical, as illustrated. Staple-gather rectangle's back panel on the vertical to wall directly below covered rectangle.

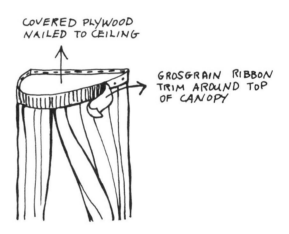

**9.** Turn one end of ribbon under ½". Staple end in place on one side where canopy meets wall. Tightly pull ribbon around front to opposite side of canopy. Turn raw edge under and staple in place. Use ribbons or tiebacks to hold fabric at side of bed.

# FABRIC WINDOWSCREENS

These add a slick touch to a room with fabric-covered walls. An added plus to this type of window treatment is that it looks pretty from the outside as well as the inside. Fabric windowscreens keep the line of the room moving, and at night, when closed, they easily conform to the wall's décor.

## YOU NEED . . .

**8 artist's wooden stretcher bars**—to create two screen frames
**Fabric**—lightweight, enough to cover both sides of both frames plus 1″ extra all around
**Tape measure**
**Marking pencil**
**Fabric shears**
**Pushpins**
**Staple gun and staples**
**White household glue**
**Ribbon or fabric trim**—finished width to equal ¾″ and enough to cover all sides of each frame
**Iron**
**Hinges and screws**
**Screwdriver**
**Optional**: 2 mini drawer pulls or unusual button heads glued onto screws

## TO MAKE IT . . .

1.

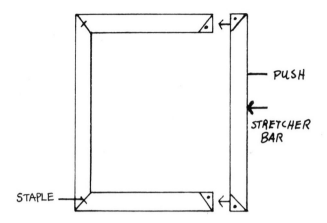

Following manufacturer's directions, push stretcher bars together to form two frames. Make sure the frames fit into your window as fabric or louver shutters would—the principle is the same. To keep frames stable, staple each corner as illustrated.

**2.** Press fabric flat. Trim off selvages. Measure, mark, and cut out four sections of fabric, each 1″ wider all around than the assembled frames.

**3.**

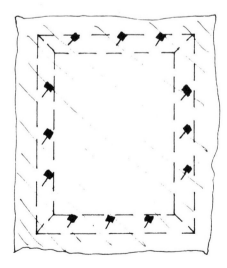

Working with one at a time, center fabric, right side up, on top of frame. Align pattern and hold fabric in place with pushpins.

**4.**

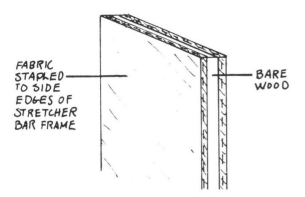

FABRIC STAPLED TO SIDE EDGES OF STRETCHER BAR FRAME

BARE WOOD

Stretch fabric over face of frame and staple along side edges as illustrated. Staple fabric as close as possible to edge of frame. Trim away excess fabric.

Flip frame to reverse side and repeat procedure. Make sure there is a channel of wood showing on all side edges of frame. This will make the trim adhere better.

**5.**

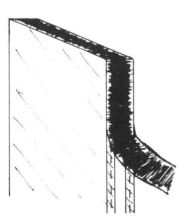

Measure, mark, and cut ribbon or fabric trim so that finished width is the exact size of edge of frame (usually ¾″). Using undiluted white household glue, adhere trim in place covering staple heads and raw edges of fabric.

**6.** Following manufacturer's directions, attach fabric screens to windows with hinges.

**7.** Finally, screw mini drawer pulls or decorative buttons to fabric windowscreens.

# TABLE RUNNERS

No-sew table runners are a quick way to create a festive look without a lot of fuss.

Any of this book's basic directions for making place mats can be enlarged upon to become table runners. Just use more fabric, more backing, and possibly washable ribbon secured to the fabric with fusible bonding web.

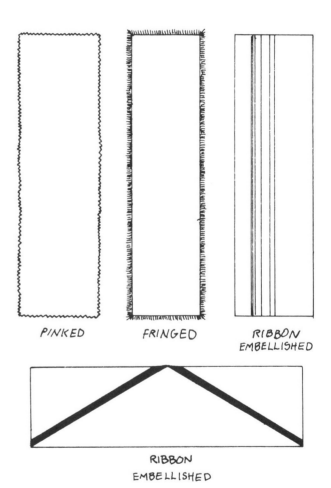

PINKED    FRINGED    RIBBON EMBELLISHED

RIBBON EMBELLISHED

Runners can either go to the table's edge or drop over it about 8″ or 10″.

The edges of table runners can be pinked, fringed, or bordered with washable ribbon held in place with fusible bonding web. Runners can also be used across tables as place mats.

Design ideas are endless.